The Singing Street

Dr James Ritchie (1908–1998) was a teacher at Norton Park School in Edinburgh before the Second World War when he began to make a collection of the games and rhymes enjoyed by his pupils. His interest in the subject grew and led to the making of a radio programme and a film, as well as the publication of two books, *The Singing Street* (1964) and *Golden City* (1965), both of which have been reissued as Mercat Classics.

The Singing Street

Scottish Children's Games, Rhymes & Sayings

James T. R. Ritchie

MERCAT PRESS
EDINBURGH
www.mercatpress.com

First published in 1964 by Oliver and Boyd
Reprinted 2000 by Mercat Press
James Thin, 53 South Bridge, Edinburgh EH1 1YS
© Margaret Longstaff and Adrian Pearce, 2000

ISBN 184183 0135

Printed and bound in Great Britain by Bell & Bain Ltd., Glasgow

CONTENTS

	Introduction	vii
1	City of Names	1
2	The Days before 1914	12
3	The Street in War and Peace	23
4	Fireside Rhymes and Sayings	54
5	The Fascination of the Pavement	70
6	Street Songs, Chants, and Recitations	94
7	Guising Ballads and Hallowe'en Ploys	113
8	The Football Muse	120
9	Art in the Street	133
	Index	137

INTRODUCTION

For over thirty years Jim Ritchie taught, officially, science and mathematics to the boys and girls of Norton Park School in Edinburgh. Unofficially he introduced them to the appreciation of art and literature, and there must be many hundreds of elderly ex-pupils who remember with affection and gratitude the unorthodox lessons of "Docky" Ritchie.

When he discovered that his pupils were more interested in their playground games than in maths, he started to collect —he was a born collector—their games and rhymes. This collection formed the basis of a programme, *The Singing Street*, which was broadcast by the Scottish Home Service in 1949. And it was in that golden age of Scottish broadcasting (before television) that his career as a radio writer began. Encouraged by that enlightened playwright and producer, Robert Kemp, a stream of poems, stories, plays and features reflected his enduring enthusiasm for everything Scottish—the language, the literature and the history, especially of his native city, Edinburgh.

His first book, *The Singing Street*, appeared in 1964, followed in 1965 by *Golden City*. These books showed him to be a worthy follower of Scott, Chambers, Leyden and Wilkie as a collector of the popular and unwritten literature of Scotland. Only Norman Douglas in his *London Street Games* had preceded him as a collector of children's games and rhymes.

In his radio plays he wrote of his heroes, Clerk Maxwell, Stevenson and Livingstone. His stories were set in what he called the "Lallans Quarter" of Edinburgh.

In the Fifties, Ritchie and his colleagues, Nigel McIsaac the painter and Raymond Townsend the photographer formed the Norton Park Group. Without official backing or encouragement they produced four films, *Happy Weekend*, *The Singing Street*, *The Gray Metropolis* (a tribute to RLS) and *The Flower and the Straw* (Victorian London as seen through the eyes of Cruikshank). These were professional works that were highly thought of by John Grierson and were widely distributed as videos.

Although he wrote poetry throughout his life, very little was published. A small volume, *A Cinema of Days*, appeared in 1951 and was praised by so severe a critic as Martin Seymour-Smith. His poems were in English and also in Scots. He made successful translations into Scots from the French of Verlaine. In 1997 *Glorious Gallimaufry* was published. It is unique in that it reconciles two of Ritchie's great passions, poetry and football. He regretted that football fans are rarely poetry readers and vice versa. In *Glorious Gallimaufry* his poems are devoted to Scottish football and footballers, chiefly of the Hearts. He was delighted when some of his poems were reprinted in the Hearts fanzine.

My friendship with Jim Ritchie began in 1947 when we met as members of a small group of writers who gathered monthly in the back room (now gone) of the Abbotsford Bar in Rose Street, Edinburgh. This group was composed of writers who contributed to Robert Kemp's radio magazine, "Chapbook", and to the Scottish literary magazines of the day, *The New Alliance* and *Chapbook*. The other members of the group were Douglas Young, Sydney Goodsir Smith, Hamish Henderson, Albert Mackie and Robert Kemp. We all wrote in Scots (or "Lallans" as it was fashionable to call it at that time), and one of the reasons for our meetings was to try to free printed Scots from the abomination of the apostrophe. The custom of scattering apostrophes over a page of Scots, like currants in a rice pudding, was a typical example of the Scots cringe which did much to encourage the false impression that Scots was not a language in its own right but a debased gutter version of English.

There is no standard spoken Scots, and we all (with the exception of Sydney Goodsir Smith) spoke, or could speak, a version of our own local dialect. Kemp was fluent in Aberdonian, Henderson knew the Scots of Perthshire, Mackie ("I'm a Lothian Nationalist") spoke Lothian Scots and Jim Ritchie spoke an unaffected Edinburgh Scots, with perhaps a trace of his ancestral Hillfoots (he was a declared admirer of Hugh Haliburton, the poet of the Ochils whose poetry he preferred to that of MacDiarmid). This led to arguments about the best way to spell the vowels of Scots. After months of debate, Albert Mackie drew up a guide sheet of our proposed new orthography. If its recommendations had been followed Scots would certainly have a maist unco look. I remember one specimen sentence was "They are aa faaan in the babbanquaa", or in English, "They are all falling into the marsh". That triple "a", representing the present participle of the verb "to faa" = "to fall", was, we agreed, a bit much.

Spoken Scots could also present difficulties. One evening Douglas Young, finding his glass empty, called the barman and ordered "Some mair". The barman, who could not imagine a bearded professorial gentleman as a Scots speaker, promptly opened the window.

For over fifty years Jim Ritchie and I met regularly and I enjoyed my many visits to his home on Corstorphine Hill with its view across to the Pentlands, for the house was a museum of modern Scottish art. For most of his adult life he had collected Scottish paintings from the time of Geikie up to the 1990s. I remember his enthusiasm as he would show me his latest acquisition. The Colourists were well represented in his collection: Peploe, Hunter, Fergusson and Cadell. Among the later generation he had a great admiration for women artists: Anne Redpath, Barbara Balmer and Elizabeth Blackadder. On one occasion, ever trusting, he allowed a bogus workman into his home. This character gaped in wonder at the huge vibrant Philipson "Rose Window" hanging on the staircase and commented; "That's a bonnie photie." And bonnie photies were indeed Jim Ritchie's delight. Perhaps his favourite was "Spring", by William McTaggart the elder, a delightful study of two wee girls in a sunny landscape. McTaggart's later version of this painting hangs in the National Gallery of Scotland.

Jim Ritchie was a born collector. Children's rhymes and games, Scottish paintings, first editions—and Scottish pottery. At a period when specimens of Scottish pottery were to be picked up in junk shops for a few shillings rather than, as now, at antique auctions, he was a familiar figure in Leith and the Old Town hunting for pieces of Portobello and Prestonpans ware. Long before Wemyss ware had become fashionable and had acquired the Royal seal of approval from the Queen Mother, he had built up an impressive collection from the Kirkcaldy kilns of the many designs of Karel Nekola. I recall the "flowers, fruit, cocks, hens and pigs" that decorated the shelves of his kitchen. His interest was mainly in the creamware of the East Coast potteries of Portobello, Prestonpans and Methven. But the more sombre self-coloured ware in rich greens and maroon glazes of the Dunmore Pottery fascinated him, and after a visit to the crumbling ruins of the pottery near Airth he began research into the history of the pottery and Dunmore House with a view to making a film. He collected stories and songs dealing with the district, its connections with Edward VII and the story of Dunmore's War in the Caribbean. But the film was never made.

Poet, playwright, collector and connoisseur, a man of many talents was Jim Ritchie.

David Fergus
Edinburgh
July 2000

1

CITY OF NAMES

Edinburgh is truly a city of names and by-names. Even her own hasn't escaped variation. Dunedin! Edina!! The Athens of the North!!! All these are more than a bit bookish. But the country folk called her "Auld Reekie"[1]; and though this name is based on the same characteristic that gets London dubbed "The Smoke," you can't help thinking it's more affectionate, just as "a lummie" sounds chummier than "a chimney fire." This tacking on of the "-ie" ending comes natural to a Scottish tongue and makes also for simplification. Streets qualified by the outlandish adjectives of Antigua, Montague, and Riego are simply pronounced "Antaigie Street," "Montaigie Street," and "Raigie Street." And in all the schools the pupils talk about "geogie [geography]," "arithie [arithmetic]," and "chemie [chemistry]", they use "blottie [blotting-paper]," hate getting an "eckie [exercise]" but look forward to going to the "lunchie [lunch-room]." This "-ie" is also brought into nearly all the names the youngsters give to the games they play.

In the matter of nicknames[2] we might as well start with Princes Street. In 1810 Marjorie Fleming observed: "Queen streat is a very gay one and so is Princes streat for all the lads and lases besides bucks and begars parade there." Princes Street has followed that pattern ever since. In the 1910s and 1920s it was almost always referred to as "The Strand" with its "Shilling Side" and its "Half-crown Side." From the 1950s on, the

---

[1] In P. Henry Bordeaux's *Fantômes d'Ecosse*, Auld Reekie appears as "La Vielle Enfumée."

[2] "I have often remarked that the present generation has lost the faculty of *giving names*. The modern streets of towns (London for a chief example) . . . are proofs of this. . . . We cannot now give so much as a *nickname*. Giving a NAME, indeed, is a poetic art: all poetry . . . is but a giving of names."—Thomas Carlyle, *Journal* (18 May 1832).

name has been "The Monkey Walk" or "The Talent Walk" —after the Teddy-boys and Teddy-girls who parade there. Sunday is a fashionable day for walking our celebrated street; and that brings us to the kirks. There's "Free St George's," of course, and then "St Mary's Cathedral" which some people know as "The Auld Claes [old clothes] Kirk." And a quarter near Church Hill where five or six kirks congregate has long been known as "Holy Corner."

Outside of Princes Street, there's "The Main Point," where Fountainbridge, Bread Street, High Riggs, Lauriston Street and the West Port meet.

↝ "Why was Tollcross?" "Because it couldn't see the Main Point."

The Kirkgate, in Leith, is called "The Channel," East Thomas Street, "Chinatown"; and the lane off Annandale Street, "The Coos' [cows'] Lane." "The Coffin Lane" is a narrow right-of-way with steps which runs along one side of the Cemetery of Old Dalry. From time immemorial the lane bore its name-plate "Coffin Lane," but in recent years this name-plate has not been renewed or replaced, which seems to show that the Town Council has a complex about coffins. "The Sweetie Lane" is an opening off Easter Road which passes under Bothwell Street and ends in a builder's yard. Formerly it was a road to the Hibernian Football Ground, and the name was inspired by Dickman's Confectionery Works:

↝ "There's an American, he must be aboot eighty-nine years o' age, he comes back regular every summer jist to see the Sweetie Lane. Ey [he] was born there. At the tap [top] was a watch-maker's until no sae long ago, and a shop that sellt skeechan [treacle beer]."

The district of Stockbridge still keeps the old name of "Stockaree," but "The Plowt" has long vanished. This was an area between the top of Cockburn Street and the Fleshmarket Close:

↝ "There was a pub there sellt corned mutton sandwiches—no [not] corned beef, mind you, corned mutton. They were great."

Then there's "Sunny Leith," as the Leithers call the port or "Dirty Leith," Edinburgh's name for it. In the capital, when someone didn't know some particular place or understand the point of some remark, one would say of him: "Ye'd think he was a foreigner from Leith." Leith itself abounds in nicknames. For Tolbooth Wynd, we have "Candles Close"; for Trafalgar Street, "Village of Trafal-gar"; the Martello Tower is the "Tally Tour"; and St Giles Street is "Back o' the Vowts [vaults]." And that wonderful thoroughfare Leith Walk has always played a great part in everyday talk:

- "As long as Leith Walk" still is a favourite simile for a glum face.

- "Hi lassies, here's fellies [fellows]!" In the 1930s, this was known as "the Leith Walk Introduction."

Then a riddle which goes back much further:

- "Why did the Castle Rock?" "Because it saw Leith Walk."

And we mustn't forget that ancient tongue-twister:

- "The Leith Police dismisseth us."

"Port o' Leith" is a common rhyming slang for "teeth," but the actual river has no name except "the Water o' Leith." A certain stretch of waterside below Canonmills Bridge has served many generations of children as a happy hunting-ground for frogs and tadpoles. It is called "Puddocky"—the exact equivalent in Scots of the Seine's "La Grenouillère." At one time most of the larger pools of the Water of Leith had their own names. This no longer appears to be the case, with the exception, perhaps of "The Cau'thron," or "The Wooden Falls," which is a swimming hole at the west end of Bell's Mill Haugh. Certainly the old "Herioters' Pool" seems to be quite forgotten, though "Currie Brig" outside the city boundary is not:

- "Now take Joe Stalin, he was as deep as Currie Brig."

Thirty or forty years ago Water of Leith Village was known as "Glaziers' Island." Before that, the popular trade had been stone-cutting, and among indwellers certain nicknames flourished—such as "Showe-showe," "Peezil," "Gags," "Wrachin," and "Shauchums."

The Figgate (or "Figgie") Burn, where it trickles down to the sea at Portobello, is christened "The Skitterie Burn."[3] Along the coast at Seafield stands a great rock on the shore, called "The Penny Bap." Hereabouts much "soorage [sewage]" goes into the sea and swimmers have always to keep a watchful eye in case they may come up against "a floating minister." Up to the 1920s there was a pond, haunted alike by elvers and urchins, and called "The Eelie Dub." It lay between Baileyfield Road and Portobello Road.

Every rock and hollow on Arthur's Seat from "The Gutted Haddie [haddock]" to "Samson's Ribs" has been named for centuries, but many may not be aware of "Napoleon's Hat," a plot of greensward near Holyrood Palace, or of "The Edinburgh Lake District"—Duddingston, Dunsapie, and St Margaret's Lochs. In snowy weather the slopes of Arthur's Seat are a Mecca for sledgers, and the following sledge-runs are the most popular: "Buffalo Brae" and "Buffalo Run," "The Banana Slide," "The Cockle Shell," and "The Quarter Mile," all in the Queen's Park; "Dead Man's Run," near St Leonard's Hill. Elsewhere in the city we have: "The Break-Neck," "The Devil's Elbow," and "The Flying Angel," all in "The Londies [London Road Gardens]"; "The Liver-Shaker," in the Braid Hills; and "The Rally Run," on Craigentinny Golf Course.

In Bruntsfield Links, "Tumblers' Hollow" is a favourite place for rolling Easter eggs; in Leith Links, "Giant's Brae" and "Lady Brae" are chosen for the same purpose. All these "heichs [heights]" and "howes [hollows]" are used for sledging, too, especially by the very young. "Grannie's Green" is a drying-green on the grassy slope between the Grassmarket and Castle Terrace.

---

[3] This name was also attached to the stream that ran alongside the old Craigentinny Golf Course.

✧ "There's a deid [dead] tree at Pirniefield and we cry it 'The Bare Lady'."

✧ "The gairdens in Hillside Crescent are ca'd 'The Plantation'."

"Brae [slope]" is a name bestowed by Edinburgh citizens on certain streets, not necessarily very steep streets, but all distinguished in some way or other: "Double Brae," where Salisbury Street branches off from Dumbiedykes Road; "Gipsy Brae," Granton Road; "Hibs' Brae," St Clair Street; "Horn Brae," North Gray's Close, High Street; "Johnnie's Brae," Lochend; "Smoky Brae," Restalrig Road South; and "The Cat's Brae," Robertson's Close, in the Pleasance. A very famous brae is "The Whale Brae" leading from Stanley Road to Newhaven. "The Cut" runs from Trinity to "the Halley," a bit of waste ground at the fishmarket and behind the Peacock Hotel, Newhaven. Newhaven is sometimes called "Carnie-town," because it has so many families of the name of Carnie. "A Bowtow" is the Newhavener's name for a Newhavener.

Like Newhaven, Musselburgh can boast names as catching as any: the "Mucklets," a walk; "Tammie Nicol Wynd," Links Street; and "Honeymoon Terrace," a big red block on the promenade. Most of the fishermen, a generation or so back, were better known by their nicknames than by their own names. These nicknames were handed down to their eldest sons, names like "Tochle," "Batchie [baker]," "Boosie," "Chows [chews tobacco]," "Feather," "Sandy Halfer," or "Touch your goblet [iron pot or pan]."

✧ "My grandfather was a fisherman and got the name of 'Tailie.' That's how it sounded. It might have been spelt 'Talie [tally].' Anyhow when I first went to school, I used to pass an old, old wife who sat at her cottage door, a bit of a busybody she was. As I toddled by, a big smile came over her face, and she'd call after me, very provokingly, 'Tailie!' This went on for one or two mornings, so I told my grandfather. 'The next time she does that,' he said, 'just you call after her, "Nervie!"' Sure enough the next morning I again got 'Tailie!' So out I came with 'Nervie!' At once that big smile vanished. She never called me 'Tailie' again. All I got was a scowl."

In the city's geography, "corners" have played a conspicuous part. Lovers still meet at "Maule's Corner," West End of Princes Street, though the name has changed to "Binns'." In Craigentinny we have "Kemp's Corner." But in the West Port, "Burke's Corner"⁴ has "passed from folk's kennin' [knowing]."

In the 1880s a makeshift iron church at Morningside Toll was locally known as "The Tin Tabernacle," and a baroquish villa in Napier Road built by a former Lord Provost, and by him called "Rockville," soon acquired the name which it still retains—"Sugar Loaf House." In the 1920s, would-be districts such as Marchmont and Morningside had attached to them the scoffing phrase "a' [all] herrin' and pianies." In former days (1920-1930) "bughouse" or "fleapit" was the name given to the nearest or favourite picture house, but nowadays "gaff" is preferred. Boys and girls go, some of them, more than twice a week:

◇   "On Friday ye go wi' your pal for a barney [fight], on Setter-day wi' your girl-friend."

Names for the different cinemas were, in the 1950s: the "Scabby Alice," the Palace; the "Aggie Kate," the State; the "Gent," the Regent; the "Cappie," the Capitol; the "Way," the Eastway; the "Alabama," or the "Alabam," the Alhambra; the "Bug House," the Victory; the "Bev," the Beverley; and the "Money Bag," the George.

◇   "They closed 'The ——' for redecoration, and a' they did was repaint the cash-box and charge ye thruppence mair."
◇   "The seats in 'The ——' have only got backs."

Some of Edinburgh's pubs have nicknames: the "Rat Trap," in Nicolson Square; the "Grave-diggers," in Henderson Terrace (opposite the cemetery); and the "Canny Man's," in Morningside Road. In the 1940s Rutherford's, on the Shore of Leith, got the name of "The Jungle" from being patronised by so many different races.

During the Second World War a land-mine was dropped

⁴ "What swarms from the Bow and Grassmarket unkennel, Burke's Corner, Main Point, Potterrow and the Vennel."—Willie Scott (1832).

between Couper Street and North Junction Street, and the derelict area has come to be called by children "The Bombies." They also refer to the throughroad of Springfield Street and Tennant Street as "The Khyber Pass," since many of the flats there are now occupied by Indian pedlars (Sikhs) and their families. Like "Irish Corner" in Old Corstorphine, this new name (and the name alone) might stick.

In the 1910s Summerside Place was pointed out as "Skippers' Alley" from the number of sea-captains residing there. Off Craigentinny Road stands a tenement that has been known as "The Shore Block" or "The Shorie" ever since the 1930s, when it rehoused people from the Shore of Leith.

"The Happy Land" is a *soubriquet* frequently applied to more notorious quarters or merrier tenements. There must be dozens of "Happy Lands" scattered up and down the city; Leith, "Sherrie [Sherriff]" Brae; Portobello, High Street, opposite Wellington Street; and Corstorphine, Victor Park Terrace. They all stem from the famous hymn "There is a Happy Land" written by Andrew Young (1807-89), the headmaster of Niddry Street School. In Scots "a land" can also mean a group of dwellings under one roof and having a common entry. The first Happy Land ("that dreadful den of burglars, thieves and profligate women") appears to have been in Leith Wynd, where it is so described in a story by Robert Leighton.[5]

"Whisky Row" is another name that has long been in use. It describes any street that houses a preponderance of publicans. It has been given to Royal Terrace in the town, and to Dudley Avenue in Leith. A vanished street in the Dean is remembered as having this title; and in the Huntly House Museum there's a water-colour of an Old Town close, not identifiable, but described on the back as "Whisky Row."

Turning to shops, "Coffee Law's" stands out distinctively in Princes Street; and a shop in any district which stocks a variety of useful goods becomes "a Johnnie-a'thing [everything]." In the baker's window may be noticed in the passing the aptly

[5] "Six Toes," in *Romances of the Old Town of Edinburgh* (1867).

realistic "scabbie heids [somerset buns]" and "fly cemeteries [fruit cakes]."

Trades, too, carry nicknames: "snabs [shoemakers]"; "wuddies [wood-workers]"; "brickies [bricklayers]." "Mill-dumpers" are factory workers. In the pageant of street life, the "Bobbie [policeman]," the "Postie [postman]," the "Milkie [milkman]," the "Parkie [park-keeper]," and the "Scaffie [scavenger]" all have long played their parts. Only "Leerie," the lamplighter, has gone his last rounds:

> Leerie, Leerie, licht the lamps
> Lang legs and crookit shanks,

a figure, perhaps not entirely forgotten, in our ghostly, sodium world.

"The Squeak" was the old name for the *Edinburgh Evening News*, and very often the columns first turned-to in this paper are those devoted to "Hatches, Matches, and Dispatches." With the elderly, "readin' the daiths" becomes an evening "must"—"Guess whae's deid!"

In Edinburgh, and in Scotland generally, there seems to be an endless number and variety of epithets for special characters,[6] such as: "Biddy Malone"; "Big Aggie"; "Black Bess"; "Black Jock"; "Black Solomon"; "Bubbly Jock"[7]; "Cairter Jock"; "Canny Harry"; "Cheerfu' Charlie"; "Clarty [dirty] Biddy"; "Clinkie [coughing] Davie"; "Creepin' Jesus"; "Daft Nell"; "Dainty Davie"; "Dirty Dick"; "Dismal Desmond"; "Douce [good-natured] Davie"; "Doubtin' Tam"; "Dreamy Daniel"; "Fat Nan"; "Fly Mickey"; "Gentle Jeanie Gray"; "Govie Dick"; "Huffie Tam"; "Handy Andy"; "Hard-hearted Hannah"; "Holy Willie"; "Hungry [greedy] Harry"; "Jenny

[6] "Last night I sat up very late reading Scott's 'History of Scotland.' An amusing narrative, clear, precise and I suppose accurate: but no more a history of Scotland than I am Pope of Rome. . . . One inference I have drawn: that the people in those days had a singular talent for nicknames: *King Toom-Tabard, Bell-the-Cat,* . . . the *Foul Raid,* the *Round-about Raid, Clean-the-Causeway,* the *Tulchan Prelates* &c. &c. Apparently there was more humour in the national mind than now."—Carlyle's *Journal* (7 Sept. 1830).

[7] "Bubbly-jock" also is Scots for "turkey."

Willox"; "Jinglin' Geordie"; "Johnnie Raw"; "Jumpin'
Jehosophat"; "Long Jonathan"; "Meddlesome Matty"; "Mim-
mou'd [-mouthed, prim] Meg"; "Pawky [sly] Jock"; "Plain
Jane"; "Pretty Polly"; "Sammy Dreep"; "Shitin' Tam";
"Silly Willy"; "Skinny Liz"; "Slim Jim"; "Slippery Sam";
"Sloppy Joe"; "Smart Alick"; "Speckie Doddie"; "Stingey
Kate"; "Straight Kate"; "Tidy Betty"; "Tiny Tim"; "Weary
Willie." And we must not forget: "Big Aggie's Man," always
accompanied by "Wee Hughie's Wife"; "Lord and Lady
Muck"; and "Mary-Ann Tea-Breid [-bread]."

The early sounds of "the cairts [carts] comin' in," which
R. L. S. found so reassuring, did not long survive the First
World War; and that early-morning character the "Cinder
Mavis [song-thrush]"—the old bent woman raking the buckets
—has now been put down. But our "Ing'n [onion] Johnnie,"
the onion-vendor who has come all the way from Brittany,
continues his smiling rounds.

The Gaelic poet Duncan Ban MacIntyre found in Ben Dorain
a theme of everlasting interest:

> A' beinn luiseanach f hailleanach
>   Mheallanach liontach,
> Gun choimeas dh'a fallaing
>   Air thalamh na Criosdachd. . . .[8]

Like an even vaster mountain, the city of names provides the
same thrill of never-ending novelty.

The language that the great majority of Edinburgh people
speak is still almost a hundred-per-cent Scots. At least, that's
what you hear in the playgrounds, in the shops, pubs, and
buses, on the football terrace, and in most colloquial talk. But
what you hear on the radio is "Morningside English"; or

---

[8] "That ben of herbs and shoots,|of clusters and fertility—|her robe has
no compare|in the lands of Christendom."—*The Songs of Duncan Ban
Macintyre*, ed. and tr. A. MacLeod, Scottish Gaelic Texts Society (1952),
ee. 2982 ff. "Donnchadh Bàn" himself was fascinated by place-names, and
in the same poem there is one short passage (ll. 3105-17) in which he
mentions Craobh na h-Ainnis, Coire Dhaingein, Coire Raineach, the
Bealach, Coire Reidh Beinn Ach-Chaladair, Cònnlon, Lurgain na Laoidhre,
Larach na Féinne, and Craig Sheilich!

"Kimly Benk [Comely Bank]"; and this same stilted speech is the only kind that is countenanced in the schools. Edinburgh children really get a rotten deal. "Keepin' a guid Scots tongue in your heid" has long been discouraged. The language of Dunbar and the makars, of Ramsay and Fergusson is curtly described as "not English"—or worse, dismissed as "slang."[9] Every time an Edinburgh child opens his mouth he has to make a thousand-and-one changes—"guid" to "good," "heid" to "head," "isnie" to "isn't," "dinnie" to "don't," "ain" to "own," "mair" to "more," "aboot" to "about," "ken" to "know," "a'" to "all," "o'" to "of" and "aye" to "always" —to say nothing of pronouncing all those "ts" and sounding all those "-ings." No wonder Scottish students don't feel at ease in English interviews, or in front of a microphone! This early interference with our natural speech[10] may also explain why Edinburgh doesn't produce lively playwrights like Sean O'Casey or Brendan Behan. As it is, the only result that education appears to achieve is the complete mucking-up of the declensions of the verbs "to do," "to see" and "to go."

✧   "Ye get tellt ye have to learn proper English,[11] or else ye'll no

---

9 This isn't the opinion of either English Scholars or visiting philologists. "Most of the sounds indicated . . . may still be heard in living dialects. I have just spent an interesting afternoon listening to the chatter of Scottish children playing in the parks and gardens, the wynds and closes, along and around the Royal Mile from Edinburgh Castle to Holyrood Palace." Simeon Potter, *Our Living Language* (1950).

10 Carlyle remarked of the "Ettrick Shepherd," James Hogg: "He is . . . able to speak naturally, which not one in a thousand is." Henry Froude, *Life of Thomas Carlyle* (1882).

11 Being familiar with Scots should be no barrier either to speaking or writing good English. Scots is good English. Carlyle, practically the inventor of modern prose, found it was the southern, not the northern, dialect that annoyed him: "*Wae, wae,*" he exclaims, "there is no word in English that will express what I feel."—*Reminiscences* (1881). Only one other writer of English can be considered side-by-side with Carlyle, namely Ruskin; and in his last writings he dwells with remarkable affection on the Scotticism "to mind." The English "to remember" couldn't sound the same deeps. Ruskin is careful, of course, to point out: "In order that you may, in the Scottish sense, 'mind' anything, there must be something to 'mind'—and then, the 'mind' to mind it."—*Praeterita* (1886).

be understood in England. But in a' thae [those] rent troubles in London, and in a' thae strikes doun there, it's aye [always] Scots that comes tae the front. Ye can hear them on T.V."

◇ "Look at thae [those] Lord Provosts o' oors when they speak. They're that Anglified ye would get your kill laughin' at them."

"No me, I'm he'rt-sorry for them."

◇ "The English like tae hear the Scots speakin' and yet some o' the Scots think the English speak better."

◇ "A [I] cun [can] understand American be"er than I cun understand English."

Satire in Auld Reekie has always been a vital part of the air we breathe. "Your common menstrallis hes [have] no tone [tune]. But *Now the Day Dawis* [dawns] and *Into Joun* [in June]. . . ."[12] "Braid Claith [broadcloth] lends fock [people] an unco heese [remarkable lift]. . . ."[13] Have we any satirists today? Only the anonymous makar appears to keep up the old standard with "East-windy, West-Endy"! It looks as though the street alone is left, and that here alone we see set up the last barricades of our language and old-time vivacity. "I will na preistis [priests] for me sing, *Dies illa, Dies ire . . .*"—that was the last will and testament of "Mr Andro Kennedy" as it rang out in the fifteenth century.[14] Nowadays, with the same sort of verve, the man in the street is just as liable to declare: "Thank God I'm an atheist!"

Of all our institutions, "the street" has proved the most loyal to our traditional character; and, of all who frequent it, none have kept so much of our old Scots culture alive, or recreated so much of it, or added so much new to it—as the children who play there.

[12] William Dunbar, "To the Merchants of Edinburgh," in *The Poems of William Dunbar*, ed. W. Mackay Mackenzie (1932), pp. 81 ff.
[13] Robert Ferguson, "Braid Claith," in *The Poems of Robert Ferguson*, ed. M. P. McDiarmid, Scottish Text Society (1954),
[14] Dunbar, *Poems*, pp. 71 ff.

2

THE DAYS BEFORE 1914

In the 1900s Edinburgh looked more like a country town. Children could walk without danger to a drinking-fountain placed at the centre of the traffic in the West End, and on that island could leisurely sample the ice-cold water from one of the iron cups that were chained there.

Apart from cable-cars, most of the vehicles were drawn by horses. Riding on the back axle of a horse-cab became a favourite pastime when the opportunity occurred. Passers-by would call out "Cull [callant, boy] ahint [behind]!" and the cabbie would flick his whip backwards to dislodge the free traveller. Some girls enjoyed this recreation almost as much as boys. Most children considered the waters of a horse's trough perfectly admirable for sailing paper boats in. And at every tram-terminus, especially during the months of May and June, a glorious, almost luxuriant, countryside would burst into being, with hedges smothered in flourish or wild roses. It is little wonder, then, that the airs and street-rhymes of these days still retained the charm of a vanished pastoral age.

A Song

❧ My name is Sweet Jenny, my age is sixteen
My father's a farmer on yonder green:
He's plenty of money to dress me in silk
But nae bonnie laddie will tak' me a walk.

I rose in the morning, I looked in the glass
I said to myself: What a handsome young lass!
My hands by my side and I gave a ha ha
But nae bonnie laddie will tak' me awa'.

A Ring-Game Song

Green peas, mutton pies
Tell me where my Jennie lies:
I'll be there before she dies
To cuddle her in my bosom.

I love Jenny over and over
I love Jenny in the clover:
I love Jenny and Jenny loves me
That's the lass that I'll ªgang wi'.   ª *go*

Flowers were very much to the fore, with "Here we Go round the Mulberry Bush," or "A Bunch of Roses She shall Wear."

Even city children in those days could name and recognise some country flowers, such as: "horse gowans [marguerites]"; "sookie soos [clover]"; "coffee [sorrel]"; "hawthorn flourish [May-blossom]"; "jaggy nettles." Four-leaf clover was much sought after in parks or at Sunday School or Band of Hope "trips."

The hats in milliners' windows were also very flowery and fruity—chiefly with gowans and cherries. As for real cherries, you could get a good handful in a "poke [bag]" for a ha'penny.

A Counting-out Rhyme

One two three four
Mary at the cottage door:
Five six seven eight
Eating cherries off a plate.

A Skipping Rhyme

Mrs Brown went to town
Riding on a pony:
When she came back
She lost her hat
And called on Miss Maloney.

The gold sovereign and half-sovereign were then working coins of the realm, and gold and silver often came together in the singing games, as in "Queen Alexandra has lost her gold ring . . .," and in:

Counting-Out Rhyme

⟡　Eetle ottle black bottle
　Eetle ottle out:
　Shining on the mantelpiece
　Like a silver threepenny-piece. . . .

A Skipping Song

⟡　One o'clock the gun went off
　I dare not stay no longer
　If I do mother will say
　Playing with the boys up yonder.

　Stockings red, garters blue,
　Trimmed all round with silver:
　A red red rose upon my head
　And a gold ring on my finger.

　Heigh-ho, my Johnnie-O,
　My bonny bonny Johnnie-O:
　The only one that I love best
　Is my bonny bonny Johnnie-O.

When the first Zeppelin sailed over Edinburgh in April 1916, that same one o'clock gun was reckoned to be the city's only anti-aircraft defence! In the days approaching 1914, though great wars were talked-of, they were not seriously expected. Battles belonged to a comic or romantic past, or the soldier set off to fight in a far country—as these three songs show:

The 42nd

⟡　Wha saw the [a]Forty-second　　　　　　[a] *Black Watch*
　Wha saw them gang awa'
　Wha saw the Forty-Second
　Mairchin' thro' the Broomielaw?

　Some o' them had [a]buits and stockin's　　　[a] *boots*
　Some o' them had [b]nane at a'　　　　　　[b] *none*
　Some o' them had kilts and sporrans
　Mairchin' thro' the Broomielaw.

My Love's a Soldier

⤞ My love's a soldier
In lands far away:
A true-he'rted laddie
Sae gallant and gay.

His ways they are so winning
And I shall wait a while
On my bonny laddie
O' the rank and file!

A day seems a month
And a month seems a year:
But my bonny laddie
He'll soon be here.

Auntie Mary

⤞ Auntie Mary
Had a canary
Up the leg o' her drawers:
It whistled for *a*hours   *a* pron. *oors*
And frichted the Boers
And won the Victoria Cross!

The attitude to the common soldier was very well summed up in the song (Tune: *Adeste fidelis*) sung then (and sung still) when two bigger children carry a smaller child between them or when two people are carrying anything long and heavy along a lobby or from one room to another:

Carry a Poor Soldier

⤞ Carry a poor soldier
Carry a poor soldier
Carry a poor soldier
Away to his grave!

The only fighting on a real and grand scale occurred on St Patrick's Day—"Scots or Irish Day"—when boys from opposing streets sallied out against each other, swinging, on the ends of long strings, paper bags filled with flour or whiting and singing:

> *Oor Side Yet*
>
> ✧ It's ^aoor side ^byet   *^a our ^b still*
>   It's oor side yet:
>   The Scots'll beat
>   The Irish yet.
>
>   ^aAfore we go   *^a before*
>   We'll let them know
>   The Scots'll beat
>   The Irish yet.

There were no picture-houses worth talking about, and the only Americanism in the language was the mocking "I reckon, guess, and calculate." All the same, "Cowboys and Indians" was one of the best-known fighting games:

> *Buffalo Bill*
>
> ✧ Buffalo Bill
>   He shoots to kill
>   Never missed
>   And he never will.

But since the turn of the century, one heard less and less, the excited cries that heralded an older game of catching others with a long length of rope: "Press Gang!" "Press Gang!"[1]

In those days there seemed to be more policemen stalking along the streets than are seen nowadays. A fat policeman was invariably nicknamed "Timothy Tightbreeks," but neither the fat nor the lean were popular. They were usually "Hieland teuchters,"[2] with "the heather still growan' between their taes [toes]." And their speech was jeered at in the couplet:

[1] Many of the bright impressionist paintings of William McTaggart (1835-1910) include children at play. And three of them are actually entitled: *The Daisy Chain* (1863), *The Press Gang* (1864), and *Hide and Seek* (1866).

[2] Gaelic is full of words which sound like "goohtch," "hoohtch," etc.; and "teuchters" seems to be an onomatopoeic Lowland Scots term of contempt for those who speak it.

◇   Camarachan chew pipe clay[3]
      In oor back-green last night!

The Bobbie also figured in more than one back-green ballad:

I Widnie be a Bobbie

◇   I [a]widnie be a Bobbie   [a] *wouldn't*
      A big fat Bobbie
      To wash my mother's [b]lobby   [b] *front hall*
      Wi' washin' [c]sodie.   [c] *soda*

      And when the sodie meltit
      I got my ear [a]skelpit   [a] *slapped*
      And tho' I [b]couldnie help it   [b] *couldn't*
      By God I felt it!

At the Cross

◇   At the Cross, at the Cross,
      Where we played at pitch-and-toss
      And the Bobbie [a]come   [a] *came*
      And chased us a' away:

      We ran and we ran
      Till we fell [a]owre a man   [a] *over*
      And that was the end
      Of the play.

But, although the boys were always coming under the Bobbie's baleful eye, the girls seldom did. They were still dancing the immemorial games of "Babylon," or "See the Robbers Passing By," or "Poor Tommy is Dead," or "We are the Rovers." On a summer's day girls found an even quieter amusement in "Chuckies." Occasionally someone dug out an old tennis racquet and both boys and girls would play at "Dully [rounders]."

Sweeties were cheap, but money was scarce; and many bairns had to be quite content with a stick of rhubarb dipped

---

[3] "Camarachan chew" is doubtless a Lowland Scots imitation of Gaelic "Cia mar tha thu 'n diugh?" (pronounced "Kimmer ha oo 'ndjew"), which means—"How are you today?" And "pipe clay" might, perhaps, be a nonsensical rhyme for Gaelic "an dé" (pronounced "'n djay"), which means "yesterday."

in a screwed-up "poke [bag]" of sugar. Few youngsters in those glorious days went about without their bottle of "sugar-allie water"—that black concoction of liquorice which was then at the height of its magical popularity:

> ✧   Sugarallie water
> Black as the *a*lum: *a chimney*
> Gether up *b*peens   *b pins*
> And ye'll a' get some!

In the days of the gold sovereign, "peens" were a favourite currency:

> ✧   A peen to see a *a*puppy-show   *a puppet-*
> A peen to see him die:
> A peen to see an auld man
> Sittin' in the sky.

Coloured fragments held in the palm of the hand made up the puppy-show; and, until the pin was paid over, all was hidden by a bit of stained glass or by a flap of paper: but the show never came up to anyone's expectation! A pin was also used to manipulate that earliest of knitting-machines, made from a "pirn [reel]" and four tacks, which devoured great quantities of "rainbow wool," and produced, for the boys, reins, and, for the girls, tumbler-stands or shoulder-shawls. In the city, golden-yellow water-melons were a sign of July. They glowed in every greengrocer's window and every wee sweetie-shop sold them in ha'penny slices. Most of the lassies' summer jewellery consisted of necklaces and bangles strung with melon seeds.

The most looked-forward-to holiday was undoubtedly "Victoria" or "Bonfire" Day:

> ✧   The Twenty-fourth of May
> Is the Queen's Birthday:
> If we *a*dinnie get a holiday   *a don't*
> We'll *b*a' run away!   *b all*

This was a great occasion. Every big street or association of smaller streets boasted a bonfire. The wood and other burnable rubbish were collected for weeks on end and guarded on the crucial nights. This evening of squibs and Catherine Wheels and Jumping Jacks was enjoyed by grown-ups as well as by younger folks.

In the schoolroom "skilly [slate pencil]" still was scratching away at sums and sentences. The girls all wore their hair long, usually in two plaits; and when we went to the seaside, we played a trick, dancing some sand about on the palms and backs of our hands:

> *The Beists in Your Heid*
>
> See a' the ᵃbeists in your ᵇheid—   ᵃ *lice* ᵇ *head*
> See the wee ᶜdrap in mine: ᶜ *drop*
> See a' the beists in your heid—
> See — there's ᵈnane in mine!   ᵈ *none*

You started off (line 1) with some sand on the palm of your hand, then (line 2) threw it into the air and caught less of it on the back of your hand; and finally (lines 3-4) repeated this, so that you finished up with no sand or "beists" at all. "Beists" might also be called "poodlers," or "bouies," or "pussie-doodles."

Most households, with girls in the family, kept in the bathroom for hair-cleansing purposes, a jam-jar filled with an infusion of "squashie [quassia] chips." Edwardian girls were rather proud of their long tresses and liked to boast they could sit down on them. And when quarrelling they would frequently shout (at each other) "Beistie-heid!" Another custom, when they fell out amongst themselves, was to turn sharply away from their old playmates and lifting their skirts up at the back would tilt their behinds in the air.

Boots were more fashionable than shoes:

> *Long Leather Laces*
>
> Long leather laces
> Only a penny a pair:
> If ye want to buy them
> Gang to George's Square.

There you'll seen an ^aauld man   ^a *old*
Sittin' on a chair
Cryin' 'Long leather laces
Only a penny a pair!'

In a time of terrible slums and monstrous over-crowding, nevertheless you could see "House to Let" signs in almost every thoroughfare. Emigration and poverty between them accounted for this.

Three Skipping Chants

❖ House to let—
Apply within:
As I go out
My neighbour comes in.

❖ House to let—
Apply within:
A woman put out
For drinking gin.

❖ House to let—
Apply within:
A woman put out
For showing her thing.

Very often, on some blissful summer's afternoon, boys on the way home from school would, for no other than goonish reasons, enter some quiet respectable tenement and shout up the well of the stair these verses:

Murder!

❖ Murder, murder, ^a polis—   ^a *police*
Three ^bfletts up!   ^b *flats*
A woman in the ^ctap flett   ^c *top*
Hit me wi' a cup.

Ma ^afit's a' bleedin'   ^a *foot*
And ma ^bheid's a' cut: ^b *head*
Murder, murder, polis—
Three fletts up!

And on every side you'd hear among the counting-out rhymes one that Walter Scott himself must often have chanted:

Eentie Teentie
- Eentie teentie figgery fell
  Ell dell doman ell
  Urky purky tarry rope
  An tan *a*toosie Jock.   *a tousled*

In the earlier years of the century the toy-shop windows and the toy-bazaars ranked almost as public spectacles. Japanese pencil-cases (price sixpence) were highly prized by both boys and girls. The 1900s were also the heyday of the Teddy Bear:

- I've got a Teddy Bear
  Blue eyes and curly hair!

This was sung in every street that was a street, to the same tune as the music hall ditty "Let's All Go down the Strand." At Eastertime, too, the confectioners' shops were startlingly attractive. Particularly fascinating were the Easter eggs with snakes in them. Another very pleasing, simple (yet cheap) toy was a little metal globe painted with the map of the world. It opened up into two hemispheres, and was found to be filled with sweeties. But these were soon eaten. The next stage was much more exciting. In the school playground you'd always see someone at it, vigorously clinking the two empty halves together to get the painted earth off, for it was rumoured that the makers were offering a big prize for the cleanest and most polished globe!

Among the catch phrases of those far-off days may be remembered:

- "Does your mother know you're out?"
- "All dressed-up, and nowhere to go!"
- "And the band played 'Believe it if you like!'"
- "I've been eating onions—don't breathe it to a soul!"
- "It's your eyes, ducky, it's your eyes!"

✧ "One foot in the grave, and the other on a banana-skin."

✧ "Edge your barrie [barrow]."

✧ "Let's all go down the Strand—and have a banana!"

✧ "Hands across the sea."   Then a favourite motto, which appeared on postcards sent to relatives who had recently emigrated, and was also used to decorate shortbread sent abroad at New-Year-time.

✧ "What's that got to do with the cars going up the Mound?" Then a very common Edinburgh rejoinder.

On the Mound the cable often failed. And somewhere along most of the other routes children were always engaged in laying pins or ha'pennies on the line to get them flattened out by the passing wheels:

✧ "A great trick of ours was to fix a bit of curved paper to a match-box and then thread a piece of string through both. The string was held by a knot. The next step was to let the string down on to the moving cable and then to see how far your match-box could travel. When it got the length o' Tollcross ye felt real good!"

3

THE STREET IN WAR AND PEACE

1. 1914-18

It was during the First World War that the cinema first began to dominate city life. Never-seeming-to-end serials ran then, such as *The Exploits of Elaine, The Diamond from the Sky, The Clutching Hand*—and to cries of "Shoat [*cave*]!" the "goodies" and the "baddies" were born. Of heroines there was quite a choice from Mary Pickford to Pearl White. But the one and only hero was Charlie Chaplin. The colourful posters pasted on the boards outside picture-houses played an important part in attracting patrons; and on a Friday evening it was with the utmost relish that eyes would scan these bills showing next week's "Charlie": Charlie in *The Champ*, Charlie in *The Count*, Charlie in *The Tramp*, or *Easy Street*, or *A Dog's Life*—and so many more! And the song on every youngster's lips was:

> ✧ The moon shines bright on Charlie Chaplin
> His boots are cracklin'
> For the want o' black'nin'
> And his baggy little trousers needin' mendin'
> Before they send him
> To the Dardanelles!

Boot-polish had not as yet ousted the cheaper "blacking" or "bleck'nin'."

It was the children, crowding the "Penny Matinees" every Saturday afternoon, who *made* Charlie. A lot of those roaring audiences were packed two in a seat: and while awaiting impatiently the first reel, they'd sing all the wartime songs, this one especially—and most tumultuously:

> ✧ 'Way down in Tennessee (without a shirt!)
> That's where I want to be (without a shirt!)
> Right on my mother's knee (without a shirt!) . . .

Chaplin was the first clown to suit his dancing to the pattern of the modern city, with its gutters and pavements, lamp-posts and walls. When he turned a street-corner at right angles, what took your breath away was the perfection of the choreography. A number of his other actions were borrowed from the street—such as flicking match-sticks or back-heeling cigarette-ends—perhaps even his "quarter-to-three feet." Very soon he had come into the skipping and counting-out rhymes, and there he has remained ever since. As a character, in every respect, he can be regarded as "The Last Gentleman in Europe."

Eevie Ivy Over

✧ Bluebells, dummie dummie shells
Evie ivy o-over!
Charlie Chaplain went to France
To teach the ladies how to dance
First your heel and then your toe,
Then ye do
Big birlie-O
Big birlie-O!

This era was also one of fantastic rumours and much-vouched-for wonders—such as the Angel of Mons, or the Russian Soldiers at Haymarket Station ("The snaw was still on their boots!")

In the winter following the death of Lord Kitchener (June 1916), a new myth was whispered from mouth to mouth in the school playgrounds—that Kitchener hadn't really been drowned, it was all arranged, he was safe in some secret hiding-place planning the ultimate victory of the Allies (like another King Arthur or Barbarossa!)

In the day sky over the city, the sight of the very occasional aircraft usually raised among the very young the cry:

✧ An airyplane
Away again![1]

[1] Cp. "An airyplane, an airyplane, Away up a 'ky," two lines from "The Nicest-Looking Warden in the A.R.P.," a song sung by Dave Willis, the "Scots comic," at the time of the Second World War. The whole phrase is really an example of "baby-talk," and belongs to the First World War.

But if it reappeared fairly soon the cry changed to:

> ✧ Sixty miles
> And back again!

Companies of soldiers were a very common sight in the streets—in training, stepping to and from barracks, or maybe it was a whole battalion on their way to France with pipes and drums playing. Here are two of the favourite street-songs inspired by the marching tunes:

> *Hieland Laddie*
> ✧ Hear the monkeys kickin' up a row—
> Tooral addie, tooral addie:
> Hear the monkeys kickin' up a row—
> Slice a dumplin', slice a dumplin'.

> *Colonel Bogey*
> ✧ Who stole the poultice from the bairn's scabby ᵃheid? *ᵃ head*
> *Ballocks!* was all the band could play
> *Ballocks!* they played it night and day
> *Ballocks!* 'twas only *Ballocks!*
> 'Twas only *Ballocks!* the band could play!

As the soldiers marched, children alongside on the pavements, would mockingly keep in step with them, chanting at the same time:

> *Left! Right!*
> ✧ I had a good job
> At thirty-five bob
> And I left! Left!
> Left! Right! Left!
> I had a good job
> At thirty-five bob
> And I left! Left!

But there was no great mockery in saying that the wages of thirty-five bob a week could be considered a good job. It certainly compared very favourably with army pay.

Before this period queues had seldom, if ever, been seen out-side shops. The word "queue" even was new to most people, and the idea of it unfamiliar, except in the story of Noah's Ark. Many shops for lack of stuff to sell closed down altogether. What caught your eye in the confectioner's were the shelves stacked round with empty sweetie-jars. Margarine almost wholly took the place of butter. It was christened "Maggy Ann," or referred to sardonically as "the holy margarine":

A Skipping Song

Away down East, away down West
Away down Alabama:
The only girl that I love best
Her name is Susy Anna.

I took her to a ball one night
And sat her down to supper:
The table fell and she fell too
And stuck her nose in the butter.

The butter, the butter
The holy margarine
Two black eyes and a jelly nose
And the rest all painted green.

"Kaiser Bill," Wilhelm II, and "Little Willie," the German Crown Prince, became figures in the everyday myth and found their way into older rhymes:

At the Cross, at the Cross,
Where the Kaiser lost his horse. . . .

and the girls started skipping to a new tune from France:

Madamemoiselle from Armenteers
Parly-voo!
She's never been kissed for sixteen years
Parly-voo!
The Prince of Wales was put in jail
For riding a horse without a tail
Inky pinkie parly-voo!

The general regimentation that was going on is reflected in this skipping-with-actions chant:

Kings & Queens

✧ Kings and Queens
And partners two
All dressed up in
Royal Blue.

Stand at ease!
Bend your knees!
Salute to the King!
Bow to the Queen!
Turn your back
To the German boy!

German boys
Are so funny:
This is the way
They earn their money:
Oopa la la
Oopa la la
Oop oop oop!

For generations the children had been dancing round in this old ring game:

✧ The big ship sails through the Eely-Alley-O,
The Eely-Alley-O, the Eely-Alley-O:
The big ship sails through the Eely-Alley-O
On the fourteenth of December.

But now the big ship had acquired a name and a fatal history:

✧ ... The big ship's name was the *Lusitania*,
The *Lusitania*, the *Lusitania*:
The big ship's name was the *Lusitania*,
E—I—*Lusitania*!

My father was the captain of the *Lusitania*,
The *Lusitania*, the *Lusitania*:
My father was the captain of the *Lusitania*,
E—I—*Lusitania*!

> The Germans sunk the *Lusitania*,
> The *Lusitania*, the *Lusitania*:
> The Germans sunk the *Lusitania*,
> E—I—*Lusitania*!

The feeling against the Germans in the opening years of the War was rather light-hearted. Up and down the town the laddies were very fond of this rhyme with its jaunty air:

> ✧ I *a*widnie be a German   *a* wouldn't
> I widnie be a spy
> I'd raither be a *b*sodger   *b* soldier
> In the *c*H.L.I.   *c* Highland Light Infantry

The H.L.I. were understood to be "Hell's Latest Invention." Just as D.S.O. signified "Dickie Shot Off." Army slang and army jokes were topical in every school playground. Everyone knew what was implied by "shot off at Mons." One of the pleasanter (and most appreciated) stories was the one about the message sent down the line. It started off as: "The Colonel's going to advance, will you send him reinforcements?" and ended up: "The Colonel's going to a dance, will you lend him three and fourpence?"

"Holy Moses, I am Dying," sung to the same tune as "What a Friend we Have in Jesus," was another song of this period—which is still highly popular with youngsters. It takes the form of an endless round and the secret of its attraction lies in the ingeniously-concealed ribaldry:

> *Holy Moses*
> ✧ Holy Moses I am dying
> Just one word before I go
> If you see a German soldier
> Stick a bayonet up his —
>
> Holy Moses I am dying
> Just one word before I go. . . .

✧ " Ye see, ye're no really sweirin'."

The First World War is also the theme of a couple of good skipping songs that are still jumped to, day in and day out. The hollowness of victory, and the rewards of fighting for your country, couldn't be made plumper or plainer:

The Night was Dark

⟡   The night was dark, the war was over
The battle-field was shed with blood
And there I spied a wounded soldier
Lying dying as he said:

"God bless my home and dear old Scotland
God bless my wife and only child
And tell the people I am dying
For I've won the Union Jack."
That's that!

Broken-hearted

⟡   Broken-hearted I wandered
At the loss of my belovéd:
He's a jolly jolly soldier
And to battle he must go.

He gave me a silver sixpence
And he broke it in two;
He gave to me the half of it
Before he went away.

He wrote me a letter
In the month of November:
And he told me not to worry
As he was coming home.

Sweet home
Marrow bone
Treacle scone
Ice-cream cone
Uncle John!

A little later, when the ink was scarcely dry on the Armistice terms (1918), the deadly flu epidemic spread across Europe—

treating friend and foe alike. That flu is perpetuated in this counting-out rhyme:

> *Red White & Blue*
> ❖ Red white and blue—
>   The cat's got the flu:
>   The dog's got the chicken-pox—
>   And so have you!

In the side-streets in 1919 small boys playing at soldiers were greatly given to marching and bawling out:

> ❖ Old soldiers never die,
>   Never die, never die:
>   Old soldiers never die—
>   They fade away. . . .

When skippers skip to "In Leicester Square there is a School," it would seem that the rhyme has in mind the same Leicester Square as in "It's a Long Way to Tipperary," so that this "bumps" chant somehow and sadly, sums up and ends the whole nightmarish epoch:

> *In Leicester Square*
> ❖ In Leicester Square there is a *school*
>   And in that school there is a *room*
>   And in that room there is a *desk*
>   And in that desk there is a *book*
>   And in that book there is a *picture*
>   And in that picture there is a *G H O S T*!

Two memorable catch-phrases of these times were:

❖ "What did *you* do in the Great War, Daddy?"

❖ "I'm laughing sandbags." A much-used metaphor for expressing security or contentment.

And, as for the rest:

❖ " 'Nuff said!"

❖ "San fairy Ann!"

II. 1918-39

The 1920s ushered in a new age which was soon made manifest in the rhymes and games of the street. Into verses that had stood unchanged for centuries the internal combustion engine now established itself, as in this double-ballie chant:

> ✧ Mother, mother, I am ill—
> Send for the doctor up the hill:
> Up the hill is far too far—
> Then we'll buy a motor car. . . .

The "Tin Lizzie [Model T Ford]" was an everyday sight, and right at the very end of the old rural skipping-song:

> ✧ Down in the valley
> Where the green grass grows. . . .

a more up-to-date note was sounded:

> Pump, pump, here comes the taxi-cab,
> Pump, pump, here comes the taxi-cab,
> Pump, pump, here comes the taxi-cab,
> Ready for the wedding at half-past three!

And in "Plainie Clappie," the oldest chant for a single ballie, was inserted this new instruction:

> Telephone
> The answer!

Ragtime tunes were heard everywhere, particularly this variation:

> ✧ Everybody's doing it,
> Doing it, doing it:
> Picking their nose and chewing it,
> Chewing it, chewing it. . . .

"Put and Take" came forward as the "craze game" of the 1920s, and "Knock Knock" reached its peak of popularity in those same years:

♦   "Knock knock!"
"Who's there?"
"Rose."
"Rose who?"
"Rows o' ᵃhoussis!"   *a houses*

♦   "Knock knock!"
"Who's there?"
"Madam."
"Madam who?"
"Ma damn troosers is fa'in' doun!"

A few of the catch-phrases of the day were:

♦   "Where do the flies go in the winter-time?"

♦   "Umpa, umpa
Stick it up your jumper!"

♦   "Hard lines
The ᵃcar lines!"   *a tram-lines*

♦   "Beaver!"

♦   "It's an old Spanish custom!"

Very often you were asked a question only for the sake of being supplied with the catch-answer,

♦   "My Grannie on her scooter!"

Which in turn brought into being another character:

♦   I stood outside the cemetery gate
By Jove it was so eerie:
And who do you think should come along
But Grandpa on his ᵃpeerie!   *a spinning-top*

Meanwhile the cinemas and picture houses had multiplied:

♦   I went to the pictures tomorrow
I took a front seat at the back. . . .

The first Westerns showed up under the jumping-ropes:

❖ Cowboy Joe
From Mexico:
Hands up, stick 'em up—
Cowboy Joe!

And many now sang to the tune of *Colonel Bogey*:

❖ *Tarzan*! was all the apes could say. . . .

After the Slump (1929) life became increasingly difficult for the many. The times are reflected in this ballad used for skipping, but very popular also as a song:

When I was Single
❖ When I was single I used a powder puff
Now I am married I ᵃcannie get the stuff.   ᵃ *can't*
Oh, it's a life, a weary, weary, life,
It's better to be single than to be a married wife!

One shouts "Mammy, give me a ᵃpiece on jam!"   ᵃ *slice of*
The other shouts "Daddy, put me in the pram!"   *bread spread*
                                                  with jam
When I was single I used to go and dance,
Now I am married I cannie get the chance.

One shouts "Mammy, put me to my bed!"
The other shouts "Daddy, scratch my wooden leg!"

The following surrealist stanza from a skipping and double-ballie chant presents a jumbled, yet highly sardonic picture of "life on the dole":

❖ My man's a millionaire
Blue eyes and curly hair
Works among the Eskimos
Having a game of dominoes—
My man's a millionaire!

The ballie chant of "Gipsy Gipsy" also belongs to the Workless Thirties, with its every verse reiterating the same idea:

✧ Couldn't afford to pay for a tent. . . .
Couldn't afford to pay for a boom. . . .
Couldn't afford to pay for a stamp. . . .

From the evidence of street-rhymes it would appear that the chief diet of the 1930s consisted of chips and chewing-gum:

Skipping with Bumps

✧ I know a Scout
Who took me out:
He gave me chips
To grease my lips. . . .

Double-Ballie

✧ P.K. chewing gum
Penny per packet:
First you chew it
Then you crack it. . . .

In the 1900s there was a street-song that went:

✧ Listen to the music in the tripe-shop
Listen to the ham-bones sing:
See the mealy ᵃpuddens jumpin' ᵇowre   ᵃ *puddings* ᵇ *over*
   the ᶜcoonter   ᶜ *counter*
And the black ᵈyins ᵉdaein' the Highland   ᵈ *ones* ᵉ *doing*
   Fling. . . .

Now it ran (to the same tune):

Murder in the Chip-Shop

✧ Last night there was murder in the chip-shop
A wee ᵃdug stole a ᵇhuddie bone: ᵃ *dog* ᵇ *haddock*
A big dug tried to take it ᶜoff him   ᶜ pron. *oaf*
And I ᵈhut him wi' a ᵉtattie scone.   ᵈ *hit* ᵉ *potato*

I ran roond to my Auntie Sarah
My Auntie Sarah ᵃwasnie in: ᵃ *wasn't*
I looked through the hole in the ᵇwindie   ᵇ *window*
She was playin' wi' a corn-beef tin.

Her teeth were lyin' on the dresser
Her hair was lyin' on the bed:
I nearly burst out laughing
She was screwin' off her ᵃain wooden leg.   ᵃ *own*

There's also a game called "Fish and Chips," which belongs
to this period, yet it goes on being played:

❖ "You a' stand in a big long line at the edge o' the kerb, and
the'll be somebody *out*, and ye have to hud oot your hands
like that, and the person that's out she goes 'Fish, fish, fish,
fish' on a' the palms, until she comes to one and says 'Chips,'
and this one has to race her to the other side o' the street. If
the 'Chips' one wins, then the one that was out has to stand
wi' her back to the winner and her arms stretched out. And
the one that won has to go under these arms and not get tug
in the passing, and if she manages, *she's out* for the next game."

After the General Strike (1926), during the years of dole and
unemployment, you could scarcely pick up the evening paper
without coming across some paragraph or other about a miner
being jailed for taking a few bits of coal from a coal-bing.
Hence the "geography questions":

❖ "What's Motherwell famous for?"
"Coal an' steel."
"An' what's Hamilton famous for?"
"Steel an' coal."

Cinema stars of the 1930s—Wallace Beery, Clark Gable,
Mae West, Shirley Temple, of the live screen—and Mickey
and Minnie Mouse, and Popeye the Sailor Man, of the anim-
ated cartoon—continued the invasion that Charlie Chaplin
had begun:

    Four Double-Ballie Chants

❖ Clark Gable
Mae West
Shirley Temple
Is the best:
Shirley Temple
Is a star:
S T A R!

❖ Popeye the sailor man
Once had a caravan:
He bought a pianna
For two-and-a-tanna
Popeye the sailor man.

♦ Mickey the Mouse is dead
He is lying in his bed:
He cut his throat with a ten-shilling note
Mickey the Mouse is dead.

♦ Minnie the Mouse came into the house
I asked her what she wanted:
A *a*piece on jam, a *b*hurl in the pram,   *a slice of bread
And that was all she wanted.   with jam   b ride*

In order to appear in these games, the star's name, besides being linked with film fame, must also come in handy for rhyming. Wallace Beery is likely to remain in this literature for a long time to come, as his name rhymes so well with that ancient and ever-popular word "bumbeleerie [bottom]." Here's a skipping-game that is a fair mixture of the old and the new:

Mary Kelly & Harry Brown

♦ Mary Kelly had a lamb
Peever peever
Sister Kelly stole that lamb
Peever eever O.

L stands for London
T stands for Town
H stands for Harry
And *B* stands for Brown.

Harry Brown of London Town
Said he'd marry me
And isn't it a blessing
To sit on Harry's knee.

Monday is my washing day
Tuesday I am done
Wednesday is my ironing day
Thursday I am done.

Friday is my shopping day
Saturday I am done
Sunday is my writing day—
And Harry never *a*come!   *a came*

Singing:
One two three a-leerie
I spy Wallace Beery
Sitting on his bumbeleerie
Kissing Shirley Temple!

This rhyme brings in "London," a key-name in Edinburgh's
street games of this period. "Babylon," so popular before 1914,
is less heard of. More for the rhyme's sake it crops up rather
unexpectedly in this skipping-song:

> ✧   Here comes Mrs Macaroni
> Riding on her snow-white pony
> Through the streets of Babylonie. . . .

And elsewhere London seemed to be ousting Babylon. Few
singing games were played more than this one:

> ✧   Up against the wall for the London Ball,
> The London Ball, the London Ball:
> Up against the wall for the London Ball,
> For the Bonny Bunch of Roses. . . .

And in the ring game "In and Out the Dusting Bluebells" the
long train of players with which the game ends, winds and
weaves about for a moment or two, and then comes to a halt
with someone announcing, like a station-master, "Lon-don!"
    A delightful chant for skipping with bumps also comes from
the 1930s. To a lovely railway rhythm the skipper journeys
to various capitals but to London first!

> *Up & Down*
> ✧   Up and down, up and down,
> All the way to London *Town*:
> Swish swosh, swish swosh,
> All the way to King's *Cross*:
> Legs swing, legs swing,
> All the way to *Berlin*:
> Heel toe, heel toe,
> All the way to *Jer-i-cho*!

Besides "London," another keyword is "China" (or "Chinese" or "Chinaman"). The land of China and its people have long exerted an extraordinary fascination, and between the Wars it was greatly exploited both by the stage and the screen (in *Chu Chin Chow* and *Dr Fu Manchu*).

There are many rhymes in which China is mentioned, as in this song, for a dancing game:

> ✧ Chinese government
> Black man's daughter. . . .

and in this one, for skipping:

> *Chinkie China*
> ✧ I live in Chinkie China
> In China far away:
> I wash my clothes in China
> For sixty cents a day.
>
> O rover, rover, rover,
> You ought to be ashamed
> To marry-arry-arry
> A boy without a name!

Both of these are sung, the second being a particularly gay little tune, often sung for its own sake. And in this song for "German Ropes," or for ballie, sung to the tune *A Bicycle Built for Two*, even Amy Johnson, who made flying history in 1930 by her solo flight to Australia, gets mixed up with China:

> ✧ Amy Johnson flew in an airyplane
> She flew to China and never came back again:
> She flew in an old Tin Lizzie
> Enough to make her dizzy:
> She looks so sweet upon the seat
> Of an airyplane built for two.

The rumba, first introduced in the 1930s, quickly caught the fancy of the greens and pavements.

Two Songs for Ring Games

❖ Mary had a little lamb
She sat it on the bunker:
Pretty Polly came along
And made it do the rumba—
Aye! Aye! Aye!
I can do the rumba.

❖ O alla tinka, to do the rumba
O alla tinka, do the
Rumba, umba umba umba Ay! . . .

And though Hitler and Mussolini were never out of the headlines in this epoch, neither of them firmly established his name in any Edinburgh games of the time. The only monster which succeeded in doing so (in 1937) is mentioned in a skipping song, and has held the street ever since:

❖ I'm the Monster of Loch Ness
My name you'll never guess
I can twirl in a ring
And do the Highland Fling
I'm the Monster of Loch Ness.

In 1939 the scene was set for the Second World War and for the moment when Big Ben would ominously strike eleven. The skippers in the street, it would seem, had long been preparing for that hour as the hero of one of their most popular chants—in that passing decade—had been the London clock:

❖ . . . Big Ben strikes *Nine*
Big Ben strikes *Ten*
Big Ben strikes *Eleven!* . . .

III. 1939-45

After war was declared the first new songs to be heard in the street were picked up by the younger people from the newly-called-up recruits to the army.

◈   I've got sixpence, jolly jolly sixpence
         I've got sixpence to last me all my life:
         I've got tuppence to lend
         And tuppence to spend
         And tuppence to send home to my wife. . . .

◈   There were fleas, fleas
         Wi' kilts and hairy knees
         In the stores, in the stores.
         There were fleas, fleas
         Wi' kilts and hairy knees
         In the Quartermaster's stores.

         My eyes are dim I cannot see
         I have not got my specs with me
         I have not got my specs with me!

         There were rats, rats
         In bowler hats and spats.

         There were tables, tables
         Wi' legs like Betty Grable's.

         There were chips, chips
         The size of battleships.

         There was coffee, coffee
         That smelt o' something awfie.

         There were kippers, kippers
         As big as bedroom slippers.

         There were lice, lice
         As big as blinking mice.

◈   They say that in the army
         The dames are mighty fine:
         You ask for Betty Grable—
         They ᵃgie ye Frankenstein.   ᵃ *give*

         Oh army life is not for me
         Gee ᵃhanna wannie go   ᵃ *and I want to*
         Sergeant won't let me go—home!

They say that in the Army
The beer is mighty fine:
You ask for old Scotch whisky—
They gie ye turpentine.

They say that in the army
The food is mighty fine:
A roll rolled off the table
And killed a pal o' mine.

They say that in the army
The fags are mighty fine:
You ask for twenty Capstan—
They gie ye five Woodbine.

They say that in the army
The beds are mighty fine:
How the heck do you know?
Ye've never slept in mine.

This skipping chant was frequently heard from the girls:

⌁ Passing the sergeant
   Ye must salute!
   Ye must salute—
   Or ye'll get no soup.

   Passing the sergeant
   Ye must salute!
   Ye must salute—
   Or ye'll get thrown oot.

While the boys sang:

⌁ Join up, join up, join up Churchill's Army
   Ten shillings a week, nothing much to eat
   Big tackety boots and blisters on your feet. . . .

The soldiers of this second war shared rather the same feelings as the 1914 "Fred Karno's Army": they didn't see themselves in a heroic light, and even the name, "Churchill's Army," in time became "Old Hitler's Army."

> ⬥ *You'll have to join, you'll have to join*
> *You'll have to join old Hitler's Army*
> Sitting on the grass, polishing the brass,
> And a' the wee fleas crawlin' up your arse. . . .

A mixture of grimness, hoping beyond hope, and more than a dash of cynicism, composed the attitude of most people to the Second World War, and some of this was expressed by the children:

> *A Ring-Game Song*
> ⬥ I can take my tea without
> Sugar, sugar . . .

> *Skipping with Bumps*
> ⬥ My teacher is *balmy*
> She wears a *tammy*
> She joined the *army*
> At the age of *one, two, three* . . .

> *Song*
> ⬥ There is a happy land
> Far far away
> Where we get bread and beans
> Three times a day:
> Ham and eggs ye never see
> [a]Nae sugar in [b]oor tea   [a] *no*   [b] *our*
> We live in misery
> Doun in Piershill Square.

Just as Armentières and the Dardanelles broke into the street-rhymes of the First World War, so the Italian campaign comes into this song—used both for skipping and for a singing game of leap-frog:

> ⬥ All over Italy
> The bugs are playing leap-frog
> One two three and over. . . .

And the desert warfare in North Africa has left this song which begins:

•• Have you heard of a tale called Ben Ghazi
    Where most of the fighting was done?
    'Twas there that a poor British Tommy
    Was shot by an old atom gun. . . .

As well as this Egyptian fragment:

•• King Farouk, King Farouk,
    *ª*Hing your ballocks on a hook. . . .   *ª hang*

"Bombers Overhead" is another game which was born out of these war-minded years. It is still played (1960):

•• "There are two lines needed to be chalked on the street and somebody's out and cries 'Man a Lifeboat!' and the rest have to have their toes touching but not crossing one of the lines, and the next cry is maybe 'Main Deck!' and you've to cross to the next lines. If the 'outer' (that's the one that's *het*) shouts 'Freeze!' ye've a' to stand still, and if ye move ye have to come out, and this goes on until only one person is left and they give the cries in the next game. Other orders ye can cry are: 'Admiral's coming!'—ye stand to attention; 'Ship sinking!'— ye go doun; 'Bombers overhead!'—ye lie doun; 'Man the guns!'—ye pretend to shoot guns; 'Submarines below!'—ye stand on the railing; 'Climb the crow's nest!'—ye climb on to somebody's back; 'Climb the rigging!'—ye stand in the middle and go like that wi' your hands; 'Man overboard!'— ye jump doon and lie on the ground; 'All hands on deck!'— ye run into the middle."

Catch-phrases of those dark warring years were:

•• "Honey pears!"
•• "Get up them stairs!"
•• "Ye cannie shove your grannie off the bus!"

The last of these eventually grew into a song:

Your Grannie & Your Other Grannie

•• Oh ye *ª*cannie shove your grannie off the bus   *ª can't*
    No ye cannie shove your grannie off the bus:
    Ye cannie shove your grannie
    For she's your mammie's mammie—
    Ye cannie shove your grannie off the bus.

Ye can shove your *other* grannie off the bus
Ye can shove your *other* grannie off the bus:
Ye can shove your *other* grannie
For she's your faither's mammie—
Ye can shove your *other* grannie off the bus.

The longer lines sometimes carry the additional phrase "Worse luck!"

And in the guising ballad "I Married me a Wife" there's one verse which brings in "spam," an article of food which was regarded in 1939-45 with the same disfavour as the margarine of 1914-18:

   ❬ I sent her for jam, O aye, O aye!
      I sent her for jam, O aye, O aye!
      I sent her for jam
      And she *a*bro't back spam—   *a brought*
      O the world must be coming to an end, O aye! . . .

Most of the rhymes about Hitler which have survived are justifiably scurrilous, and this verse condenses the kind of history he tried to make:

   ❬ Julius Caesar did a beezer
      On the coast of France:
      Hitler tried to do the same—
      But did it in his pants.

IV. 1945-64

When the War ended and the men (and women) returned to "Civvy Street," the housing shortage was most acute. A number of citizens in desperation knocked together some sort of shack or home on any bit of land that looked waste, vacant and handy. They were the "Squa'ers [squatters]." Parodies of "I Love a Lassie" have long been common, the "Sausage Song" being one of them. In the middle of the 1940s this new parody was often sung at "Hallowe'en Guising" or in "Backgreen Concerts":

I Love a Cookie

◇ I love a *^a*cookie   *^a a kind of bun*
A Co'perative cookie
A *^b*haill big cookie to *^c*masel: *^b whole   ^c myself*
Ye squeeze oot the cream
And hear the cookie scream—
Mary, my Scots bluebell!

I love a cabbage
A Co'perative cabbage
A haill big cabbage to masel
Ye cut oot the *^a*hairt   *^a heart*
And *^b*gie it to your *^c*tairt   *^b give   ^c tart, girl-friend*
Mary my Scots bluebell!

I love an *^a*aipple   *^a apple*
A Co'perative aipple
A haill big aipple to masel:
Ye cut it up in *^b*qua'ers   *^b quarters*
And gie it to the *^c*squa'ers—   *^c squatters*
Mary, my Scots bluebell!

I love an *^a*ingan   *^a onion*
A Co'perative ingan
A haill big ingan to masel:
Ye fry it wi' a sausage
And hear the ingan singan'—
Mary, my Scots bluebell!

As the peace-time standards were slowly restored, and the street-lights shone more brilliantly, the new stars of the cinema began to shine too—mingled and mixed up with the older heroes and heroines:

A Ballie Chant

◇ Eachy peachy pearly plum
I spy Tom Thumb—
Tom Thumb in the wood:
I spy Robin Hood—
Robin Hood in the cellar;
I spy Cinderella—
Cinderella at the ball:
I spy Henry Hall—

Henry Hall in the house:
I spy Mickey Mouse—
Mickey Mouse in the stable:
I spy Betty Grable—
Betty Grable in a hurry:
I spy Ruby Murray—
Ruby Murray is a star:
S T A R!

A Skipping Song

⬥ Marilyn Monroe
Fell in the snow:
Her skirts blew up
And the boys cried "Oh!"

A Ring-Game Song

⬥ I'm Shirley Temple and I've got curly hair
I've got dimples and wear my skirts up there:
I'm no able to do my Betty Grable
I'm Shirley Temple and I've got curly hair!
Salomé, Salomé, you can do Salomé,
Hands up there, skirts down there:
You can do Salomé!

Skiffle groups became the rage, and Teddy-boys ambled into history—along with "rock 'n' roll":

Two Songs

⬥ For we are the Teds o' the Kirkgate
We're the champs at the old rock 'n' roll:
We go to the Palais
Take them on in an alley
And get battered and sent up the pole.

⬥ Rock 'n' roll is over
And Tommy Steele is dead:
He wants to go to Heaven
With a crown upon his head.

The Lord said: "No!
You'll have to go below:
There's only room for Elvis
And his wee banjo!"

The person most responsible for the Teddy-boy might be Beau Brummell, for the Teddy-boy's rig-out is surely a modern expression of the Philosophy of Dandyism—which will probably evolve further. In the real Edwardian times it had come to a sort of dead end—in mere pointed shoes and fancy waistcoats—which were sported by certain hangers-on of racing and gambling. On this subject of clothes, *Sartor Resartus* perhaps should be our Bible, to remind us that "decoration" is "the first spiritual want."

The attitude of "the street" to "the polis [police]" has remained more or less unchanged throughout half a century and more. Instead of "I wish I was a Bobbie," sung so gleefully before 1914, the song in the 1950s becomes:

> ✧ I was standing at the corner
> With my razor and chain:
> Along came a copper
> And he took my name.
> He grabbed me by the collar
> Of my gaberdine coat:
> I took out my razor
> And slit his throat.

Though the rhythm is genuine rock'n'roll, the conclusion is false, a ridiculous exaggeration, sheer bravado. The Teddy-boy, to defend his dandyism, is more likely to use a rhyme than a razor:

> ✧ Suits the wearer
> Not the starer!

And anyone who grabs him by the lapel of his gaberdine coat would more likely be met with:

> ✧ Watch the gab, Scab!
> Cost a guinea, Skinnie!
> ᵃNo a ᵇtattie, Fattie!   *ᵃ [I'm] not ᵇ potato*

Another humorous fighting phrase is:

> ✧ "Hud ma ᵃjaicket, ᵇGlaiket!"   *ᵃ jacket ᵇ Senseless*

With the coming of television, T.V. personalities and T.V. programmes were worked into songs and games; and the older rumba is countered by the newer twist.

A Skipping Chant

Bronco Lane had a pain—
So they sent for Wagon Train:
Wagon Train was no good—
So they sent for Robin Hood:
Robin Hood lost a bow—
So they sent for Ivanhoe:
Ivanhoe killed a man—
So they sent for Big Cheyenne:
Big Cheyenne was having tea—
So they sent for Laramie:
Laramie lost its cargo—
So they sent for Wells Fargo:
Wells Fargo lost a hunter—
So they sent for Billy Bunter:
Billy Bunter was too large—
So they sent for I'm in Charge:
I'm in Charge was too thin—
So they sent for Rin-tin-tin:
Rin-tin-tin was having dinner—
So they sent for Yul Brynner:
Yul Brynner had no hair—
So they sent for Fred Astaire:
Fred Astaire liked to dance and sing—
So they sent for Dave King:
Dave King had a hole in his pocket—
So they sent for Davey Crocket:
Davey Crocket signed a treaty—
So they sent for Dear Old Beattie:
Dear Old Beattie couldn't care two hoots—
So they sent for Excused Boots:
Excused Boots loved eating fudge—
So they sent for Dear Old Snudge:
Dear Old Snudge broke his jaw—
So they sent for Gun Law:
Gun Law got scared and ran—
So they sent for Lawman:
Lawman took very sick—
So they sent for Maverick:

MAVERICK was down in heart—
So they sent for BROTHER BART:
BROTHER BART missed his train—
So poor old BRONCO had to keep his pain!

A Song

⟡ Perry Como
Uses Omo
Every day
And his nightshirts
Are all white shirts
So they say
So be wise friends
Take advice friends
Use this Omo
Every day
And your nightshirts
Will be white shirts
Every day

A Skipping Chant (1962)

⟡ Ena Sharples, how about a date?
Meet me at the Rovers' at half-past eight:
You buy the milk stouts, I'll buy the crisps,
You'll do the rumba, and I'll do the twist.

Alongside "Cowboys and Indians" is ranged the same game with a new name, "Japs and Americans."

During the 1950s there was a remarkable revival of Valentines. An enormous number of these verses are in circulation and the Jack (or Jill) of all such rhymes must surely be:

⟡ Roses are red
Violets are blue
Honey is sweet
And so are you.

But in every decade dozens of new variations appear; and here are two of today's:

A Valentine

❖ Roses are red
Bananas are yellow:
I want you
For my steady fellow.

A Double Ballie Chant

❖ Roses are red
Violets are blue:
Open that safe
Or I'll shoot you!

There are also a great many couplets for inscribing on the outsides of envelopes carrying Valentines:

❖ ᵃPostie, Postie, do your duty: *ᵃ postman*
Take this to my green-eyed beauty.

❖ Postie, Postie, do your stuff:
Take this to my wee cream puff.

❖ Postie, Postie, don't be slow:
Be like Elvis, go-man-go!

❖ Postie, Postie, do not tarry:
Be like Steptoe, use a ᵃbarrie.   *ᵃ barrow*

As for the verses for writing on cards everybody is very busy the week before the 14th of February either inventing them or collecting them.

❖ I love your hugs
I love your kisses:
I hope some day
We'll be Mr and Mrs.

❖ My dearest darling Ducky
Your neck is ᵃawfie mucky: *ᵃ awfully*
But never mind, you will be mine,
My dearest darling Ducky.

Despite their liking of "zing," and their way of admiring anybody "who has what it takes," the 1960s may well see the introduction of more Victoriana.

Some of the catch-phrases of the 1950s were:

- ⋄ "Couldn't care less!"

- ⋄ "Fair enough."

- ⋄ "Not to worry."

Early in the 1960s another catch-phrase was:

- ⋄ "It went like a bomb."

In the form of skipping, known as "bumps," the chanting of the verse is halted at certain words, so that these words get a special emphasis. In this way the cleverest tension is built up:

- ⋄ In the *dark dark* world
  There's a *dark dark* country
  In the *dark dark* country
  There's a *dark dark* wood
  In the *dark dark* wood
  There's a *dark dark* ᵃhouse   ᵃ pron. *hooss*
  In the *dark dark* house
  There is a man trying to mend a fuse!

But whether the skippers in the street are darkly hinting at the global situation or merely enjoying a joke—or both—is anybody's guess.

One established fact of the 1960s is that "fish and chips" no longer continues to be the common order in the "chippie [chip shop]." The original fish supper (going back to the 1890s) was called a "tuppenny tight'ner," and for a long time the usual way of insulting someone who showed you the family photograph was to enquire: "Whae's that posin' like a fish supper?" "Pie suppers" come first now, because they are cheapest, "pudding suppers" come next, then "fish," and lastly, for the *nouveau affluence*, "chicken suppers."

Among teenagers in 1963, the greatest new craze was for the musical entertainment supplied by "The Beatles." Now that picture houses have dropped in importance, and the creation of screen stars has rather fallen off, the coming to the top of such teenage idols, is only to be expected:

♦   The Beatles are four in group
    Paul, George, John and Ringo:
    To show my mum was such a fan
    She even missed the bingo!

♦   We four lads from Liverpool are:
    Paul in a taxi, John in a car,
    George on a scooter, tootin' his hooter,
    Following Ringo Starr!

♦   John, George, Ringo, and Paul
    Have some hair between them all!

Whether the Beatles will stay in the street rhymes is a question for time. Besides rhymes (and hair cuts), "Beatlemania" takes up jackets—as well as jokes.

♦   "A gote [I got] ma Beatle jaicket last night. Ma faither say'd: 'Is that what ye want for y'ur Christmas?' A didnie believe 'm, but he went and bote [bought] me yin. A wore it last night. Pure black wi' a red band doun the middle. It's gote wee gold buttons oan [on] it and a wee chain at the tope [top]. And gold buttons oan the cuffs. Ma mother say'd: 'It's mair like the army,' so A'm gaun [going] tae swop it this efternin [afternoon]."

♦   "What did The Searchers find under The Rolling Stones?"
    "The Beatles."

♦   "What do the Beatles cut their hair wi'?"
    "Clipshears [earwigs]."

The Beatles serve to remind us how often and abruptly the changes keep ringing in the street. The newest fashions come in, the oldest customs die out. Our May "Bonfire Night" is no longer, for young and old, the grand affair it once was. Modern roads, traffic, and summer time have all conspired to discourage this ancientest of fire festivals.

⋄ "We cannie have a bonie [bonfire] in oor street because there's the bingo, and a' the cars are there, and the windies [windows] might get it."

⋄ "We aye [always] have a bonie in Chinatown [East Thomas Street]."

The "fifth of November," quite uncelebrated in the days before 1914, has now smooled its way into the northern calendar. At the very least, it provides a second opportunity in the year for setting off "bangers."

The trams and the tram-lines have gone too—and all the pastimes associated with them. "Lighted galleons," someone once described our trams as: and in that picture we see them again. But there's nothing so good as a rhyme for restoring a ghost. In triumph, even the old cable days, can come rumbling back:

⋄ No more clay pipes
   Nothing but cigars—
   Now that I'm a driver
   On the tramway cars!

4

FIRESIDE RHYMES AND SAYINGS

Rhymes enter our lives with the first lullabies we hear. And more and more rhymes follow as we grow older. They mount up and remain in our minds, so that in daily living hardly a moment passes that can't be matched with a song, or a verse, or a couplet or at least some saying with wit or poetry in it.

In most Edinburgh households the old Scots nursery rhymes still keep a firm hold. This one is for "a greetin' [crying] bairn":

> ⟡ Alie balie alie balie bee
> Sittin' on your mammie's knee:
> Greetin' for anither [a]bawbee   *a halfpenny*
> To buy sugar candy.

And this one is sung "when the bairn's no weel":

> ⟡ Cockie Bendie's lyin' [a]seik   *a sick*
> Guess ye what'll mend him:
> Twenty kisses in a [b]cloot—   *b cloth*
> Lassie, will ye send them?

The next is often recited by a mother who has had to bandage her child's eye with a big handkerchief, so as to encourage the "patient" to keep the bandage on.

> ⟡ Blinkin' Jock the cobbler
> He had a blinkin' [a]ee . . .   *a eye*

This one is said while "dancin' the bairn on your knee":

> ⟡ Cripple Dick upon a stick
> Sandy on a [a]soo   *a sow*
> Ride a mile to Berwick, John
> To buy a [b]pund o' [c]oo.   *b pound c wool*

This one is said while getting the bairn ready for bed:

⋄ Diddle diddle dumpling my son John
   Went to bed with his trousers on,
   One shoe off and one shoe on
   Diddle diddle dumpling my son John.

And this one is said when drying the bairn after a bath:

⋄ I had a little pony
   Its name was Dapple Gray
   I lent it to a lady
   To ride a mile away.

   She ᵃwheeped him, she lashed him   *ᵃ whipped*
   She rode him through the mire,
   I would not lend my pony now
   For any lady's hire.

These two are chanted while "buffin' [patting] the bairn's bare feet wi' the palm o' your hand":

⋄ Lucy Locket had a pocket—
   Guess ye what was in it?
   Sugar ᵃbools and wee toadstools—   *ᵃ balls*
   That was what was in it.

⋄ Can a monkey climb a tree?
   Yes it can, yes it can, yes it can!
   Can a ᵃpowny ᵇspeil a ᶜbrae   *ᵃ pony ᵇ climb ᶜ slope*
   Yes it can, yes it can, yes it can!

While singing "Ride a Cock Horse," you "dance the bairn up and down on your knee, or else you take his hands, and he rides up and down on the foot of one of your crossed legs":

⋄ Ride a cock horse
   To Banbury Cross
   To see a white lady
   Ride on a white horse.

Rings on her fingers
And bells on her toes
She shall have music
Wherever she goes.

"Katie Beardie" is sung while "walkin' the bairn":

♦　Katie Beardie had a ^acoo   *a cow*
　　It was black aboot the ^bmou':   *b mouth*
　　^cWasnie that a dainty coo?   *c wasn't*
　　Dance, Katie Beardie!

　　Katie Beardie had a hen
　　It could toddle ^abut and ben: *a out and in*
　　Wasnie that a dainty hen?
　　Dance, Katie Beardie!

Then there are many versions of the rhymes which bring into play a child's brow, eyes, nose, and mouth:

♦　^aChap at the door   *a knock*
　　^bKeek in   *b peep*
　　Lift the ^csneck   *c latch*
　　And walk in.

♦　Knock at the door
　　Keek in
　　Lift the sneck
　　And wipe your feet
　　And walk in.

♦　Knock at the door
　　Peep in
　　Lift the latch
　　And walk in.

♦　Knock at the door
　　Look in
　　Ring the bell
　　And walk in.

♦　Rap at the door. . . .

When a bairn is being coaxed to sup from a spoon, this bit of imagination often proves useful:

> ✧ Doun Craig's Close
> And into Pudden Market!

"Craig" is a common Scots surname, and a "close" is a narrow entry or passageway between two houses: but a "craig" is also Scots for "neck," and so "Craig's Close" means "the throat." "Pudden" means "pudding": but it is also the Scots for "stomach"; and "Pudden Market" needs no explanation.

During the Victorian and Edwardian periods, most children, when they were tucked in bed at night, were taught to say this prayer:

> ✧ This night when I lie down to sleep,
> I pray thee, Lord, my soul to keep:
> If I should die before I wake,
> I pray thee, Lord, my soul to take.

Almost all the children in working-class homes still (1964) learn this prayer. It stands alone. A very few say:

> ✧ Matthew, Mark, Luke and John
> Bless the bed that I lie on:
> Four corners to my bed,
> Five little angels there be spread:
> Two at my head, two at my feet,
> One at my heart my soul to keep.

But although this supplication is not so well-known for praying, there are nearly a dozen chants for skipping, in which it is parodied:

> ✧ Matthew, Mark, Luke, and John
> Next person carry on. . . .

As for "Wee Willie Winkie," this not-so-old bedtime classic is not ours alone. From Scotland it has spread to almost every country in the world. That old kitchen favourite "Castles in the Air,"[1] perhaps more correctly "Castles in the Fire," is rather less often sung, and you wonder what will happen to it in a future of smokeless zones and coalless hearths.

Even in the 1920s this curious threat to the "waukrife [sleepless] bairn" still lingered on in some households:

> ❖ If ye [a]dinnie go to sleep   [a] *don't*
>   I'll get Chrystie Cleik.

"Chrystie Cleik" is said to have been an ogre who "cleiked [hooked] ye up and ate ye."

Children are rather fond of eerie stories, and even today no-one excels the grandma of the household in telling stories of that kind or any other kind:

> ❖ There was a crookit man
>   And he walked a crookit mile:
>   He found a crookit sixpence
>   Beside a crookit style:
>   He bought a crookit cat
>   And it caught a crookit [a]mouse   [a] pron. *mooss*
>   And they a' lived thegither
>   In a wee crookit [b]house.   [b] pron. *hooss*

And if the grandmother doesn't point out the mark of "Peter's thumb" on a "huddie [haddock]," then who else will?

The modern grandmother is supposed to dislike being called "Grannie," but this dislike goes back a long time. Even Burns was careful in the matter, for in "Hallowe'en" he wrote:

> I've heard my *reverend* grannie say. . . .

The grandmother has always been a considerable character in the Scottish family. It is *her* age that the grandchild is first interested in, usually to be told:

> ❖ "I'm as old as my little finger and a wee bit older than my teeth."

[1] By James Ballantine (1808-77), "who laughingly bore the honour of being the poet-laureate of the West Port."—Alison Hay Dunlop, *Anent Old Edinburgh* (1890).

n return, it is rather interesting to hear, from her, something
prophetic about yourself—unless you happened to be born on
Wednesday:

> ✧ Monday's bairn is fair of face,
> Tuesday's bairn is full of grace,
> Wednesday's bairn is full of woe,
> Thursday's bairn has far to go,
> Friday's bairn is loving and giving,
> Saturday's bairn works hard for a living:
> But the bairn that's born on the Sabbath day
> Is blythe and bonnie, good and gay.

Great-grandmothers have never been so plentiful as they are
now. Some of them can well remember the "Fast Days," now
the "Spring Holiday" and the "Autumn Holiday." These two
last are Monday holidays, but the Fast Days were celebrated
exclusively on Thursdays. An important "fair" that used to be
held in the Grassmarket was "All-Hallow Fair." A great selling
of horses took place there, and the side-shows or "penny gaffs"
attracted much custom. So did the many stalls famous for long
gingerbread snaps, for "aipple pirlie-pigs [earthenware money-
banks, in the form of an apple, with a slot]" that cost a penny
each, and for "stookie [stucco] statuettes o' Willie Gladstone."

As Valentines have returned, so may Grandma's "lockets,"
never looked-at without saying:

> ✧ Keep hair,
> Keep care!

And here are some of the remedies that Great-grandmother
was brought up on:

✧ For a stye in the eye: to rub it with a gold ring or a black cat's
tail.

✧ For a cut and bleeding finger: to wrap round it a spider's web,
which would probably be obtained from the coal-cellar.

✧ For a burnt finger: to hold it up to the ribs of a hot fire.

✧ For a sore throat: at bedtime, to wrap your stocking round
your neck.

Most grandmothers and great-grandmothers still believe in washing clothes at home, and here is a washing calendar which records how they were brought up to think of anybody who washed on each particular week day:

> ✧   Them that wash on Monday
>   Have a' the week to dry;
>   Them that wash on Tuesday
>   Have nothing to do but cry;
>   Them that wash on Wednesday
>   They wash for shame;
>   And them that wash on Thursday
>   Are very much the same.
>   Them that wash on Friday,
>   They wash for need:
>   But them that wash on Setterday
>   Are dirty sluts indeed.

Hallow-Fair Week was the first week in November; and in the old days it was "the one week in the year when naebody washed their claes [clothes], for the weather that week was aye [always] sae mauchie [clammy], wi' nae drouth [drought] for dryin'."

From the older folks, children still imbibe many well-known superstitions, such as that:

✧   An itchy nose is a sign "that ye're gaun to be crossed, vexed, or kissed."

✧   A spark jumping out of the fire means "Sharp News."

✧   A tissue of soot wavering on the burning coals foretells a "Visit from a Stranger."

✧   Two spoons in a saucer, or "falling *up* the stair," means an "Approaching Marriage."

✧   A dog heard whining at night forecasts a "Funeral."

✧   A moth alighting on you means a "Letter."

Another greatly honoured and most respected lodger in the Scottish home is the family cat or "Cheetie-Pussie-Cattie-O":

⟡   Pussie at the fireside
     Suppin' pease *a*brose: *a porridge*
     Down came a cinder
     And burnt Pussie's nose.

     "Oh," said Pussie,
     "That's no fair!"
     "Oh," said the cinder,
     "You *a*shouldnie been there!"   *a shouldn't [have]*

And, when they purr, most cats in the Lothians, and all cats in Edinburgh, are still understood to be uttering the words: "Threids [threads] and thrums [thread-ends], threids and thrums!"

Some of the many roles that the cat plays in the popular imagination are indicated in the following phrases:

⟡   "A Cat's Game": one that nobody wins.

⟡   "A Cat's Lick": a very hasty or inadequate face-wash.

⟡   "A Cats' Concert": several voices singing (or instruments being played) all out of tune.

⟡   "A Cats' Concert" of cats is, of course, a "cattie-wowin' [-mewing]."

⟡   "Cat's Meat": the matter sometimes found, on waking, in the corners of your eyes.

⟡   "Cats' Union": supposed to be where the cats are bound for when they go out at night.

By comparison the dog appears rarely. But:

⟡   The Lion and the Unicorn
     Were fighting for the *a*Croun: *a Crown*
     Up jumped the wee *b*dug   *b dog*
     And knocked them baith *c*doun.   *c down*

     Some got white bread
     And some got *a*broun   *a brown*
     But the Lion beat the Unicorn
     A' through the *b*toun.   *b town*

And:

✧ "If a bairn's cross, he's often told: 'You've a wee black dug [dog] up your back'—and very often he'll stop greetin' [crying] to look for it."

Then there are the rain-rhymes, snow-rhymes, and weather-rhymes, which nearly all are learnt in the home when the child is very young:

Rain-Rhymes

✧ Rain, rain, go to Spain
And never never come back again!

✧ Rain, rain, go away
Come again another day.

✧ Rainy, rainy, *a*rattlestanes   *a* . . . *stones*
*b*Dinnie rain on me   *b don't*
Rain on Johnnie Groats' *c*House   *c* pron. *hoos*
Far across the sea.

✧ Rain before seven
Fair before eleven.

Snow-Rhyme

✧ The folk in the East
Are pluckin' their geese
And sendin' their feathers
Tae oor *a*toun.   *a town*

Red Skies

✧ A red sky at night
Is the shepherd's delight.

A red sky in the morning
Is the shepherd's warning.

Spring Frost

✧ As the day len'thens
The cold stren'thens.

After the longest night daylight is reckoned as lengthening by a "cock's stride" every evening.

There is also another weather-rhyme which says:

> ⟡ What Friday gets
> Friday keeps:
> What Setterday wants
> Setterday seeks.

Here are two other sayings about Friday:

⟡ "Very often on a Friday, if it rains, it rains a' day: but on Setterday it usually dries up about six o'clock at night—and that's true."

⟡ "Friday rules the week."

On a cloudy day, you may hear somebody say:

⟡ "If there's enough blue in the sky to patch a Dutchman's breeks, then the sun'll break through."

Two Household Rhymes

⟡ A mole ^aaboon your ^bbraith   *a above* *b breath*
   Ye'll be rich afore your ^cdaith.   *c death*

⟡ ^aGantin's wantin'   *a yawning*
   Sleep, meat,
   Or diversion.

Toasts

⟡ Here's tae us!
   Wha's like us?
   —Damned few!

⟡ Here's to you and yours
   And here's to me and mine:
   And if ever me and mine
   Meets in wi' you and yours
   Me and mine'll be as ^aguid   *a good*
   To you and yours
   As you and yours
   Has been to me and mine.

⟡ North, South,
  East, West,
  ^aHame's best.   *a home's*

An Admonition

⟡ Patience is a virtue—
  Deny it if you can—
  Seldom in a woman
  But never in a man!

Colours

⟡ Red and green should never be seen
  Except on a maid and an Irish colleen.

⟡ Red and green should never be seen
  Except on the head of an Irish Queen.

A Bride should Wear . . .

⟡ Something old
  Something new
  Something borrowed
  Something blue.

Green is not usually regarded as a lucky colour. But:

⟡ "Long ago, when a younger sister or brother got married, the
  unmarried elder sister or brother wore a green garter at the
  wedding."

Another Saying

⟡ Happy is the bride that the sun shines on:
  Happy is the corpse that the rain rains on.

Luck

⟡ There's a new moon—
  Touch half-a-croun!

⟡ See a ^apeen   *a pin*
  Pick it up:
  A' that day
  You'll have guid luck.

A Cuppie Tea

✧ Unless the water be boiling
And the tea-pot hot
A cup of good tea
Can never be got.

When entertaining a visitor, a housewife may ask, "Would you rather have high tea or low tea?" and then holds the tea-pot high or low, whichever the guest chooses.

If a child has been up to some mischief, the mother's warning is nearly always couched in this fashion:

✧ "A wee bird has been telling me. . . ."

✧ "A wee fairy has been telling me. . . ."

✧ "The angels told me. . . ."

✧ "Jock McCrony told me. . . ."

Instead of saying "I'll report you to the police," a neighbour might say:

✧ "I'm going to tell wee Jock Murphy."

When a child asks, "Where's my mammie?" he's often told:

✧ "She's away to jine [join] the sodgers [soldiers]."

✧ "She's away to the Foot o' the Walk to find out the time."

✧ "She's away to get a hurl [ride] in the wheelbarrie [barrow]."

✧ "She's away to marry a black man"—or, in the 1940s, "a Pole."

His daddie's absence may be explained by saying:

✧ "He's away to London to buy ye a bell"—or "a dug [dog]."

✧ "He's away to join the Foreign Legion."

Young people asking for money may be answered:

✧ "I'm no made o' money."

✧ "I'm no made o' the Mint."

✧ "I havenie [haven't] a bank account at the Mint."

✧ "Money disnie growe [doesn't grow] on trees."

✧ "I'm no Andrie Carnegie's wife."

✧ "I'm no a walkin' bank."

✧ "Your faither works in the mill—he disnie [doesn't] own it."

✧ "Where have *I* thruppence? You'll have to break into a bank."

✧ "What dae ye think I am—the Bank o' Monte Carlo?"

There are a great many household expressions, exclamations, and proverbs:

✧ "A hungry man's an angry man."

✧ "A good soldier never looks behind." An excuse offered by anyone who has neglected to polish or clean the heels of his shoes.

✧ "Ach to Denny!"

✧ "Anybody that sees ye in daylight'll no run away wi' ye in the dark."

✧ "A richt Auntie Beanie": someone very old-fashioned in dress or manner or both.

✧ "Away to Bamff and gether buckies [whelks]!"

✧ "Aye ahint [always behind], like the coo's tail!"

✧ "Back to auld claes [old clothes] and parritch [porridge]!" Often said on getting back home from a holiday.

✧ "Bocht [bought] wit's the best wit." Wisdom from experience.

✧ "Buy your bones where you buy your beef!"

✧ "Eat your beef and tatties [potatoes] first, like the folk in Aberlady!" Said when the soup is too hot to sup.

✧ "Everybody's queer except you and me—and sometimes *you*'re queer."

✧ "Everything's mixed with mercy."

✧ "Every time you sigh, you take a day off your life."

✧ "Feed the brute!"

✧ "*F L Y* spells 'Fife'."

- "Forpit o' tatties [potatoes]." A "forpit" is the fourth part of a peck.

- "Geedle Godle!"

- "Good Gordon Highlanders!"

- "Hash-ma-gundie." A bad job, or anyone who makes a hash of anything.

- "He never sees green cheese but his een reels [eyes roll]."

- "He'd speir [question] the erse oot [out of] a wheel-barrie [. . . -barrow]."

- "Hey for the day o' the morn [tomorrow]!"

- "If I cannie [can't] find ma slippers, ma mother might say, 'They're no hingin' [hanging] up there,' and she'd point to her nose; or if I said, 'Where's my shoes?' she'd maybe answer, 'Hingin' to ma nose shouting "Tarzan!" and the same for my gloves, 'Hingin' to the end o' my nose shouting "Tarzan!" ' "

- "It has a way o' its ain, like the man's mither."

- "It's a fine ham-a-huddie [haddock masquerading as ham]- but it'll no fry": It's a fine tale but it can't be believed.

- "Kill the auld [old] first!"

- "Lord God o' the Hielands!" or "Lord Bugger-Magee!"

- "Never put anything smaller in your ear than your elbow."

- "Paddy's blanket" (or "the Irishman's blanket"): any blanket or sheet which is so short that you're tempted to cut a portion off the bottom and sew it on to the top.

- "Paddy's Market": any room that's in a confused state.

- "Stick your fingers in your een [eyes] and mak' starlight." In the days of gas-light, when most people were not nearly so well-off as nowadays, this was commonly the answer given to any of the younger folk of the household who asked, "Can I put on the light?"

- "Soor dook": buttermilk.

- "Sparrowfart": dawn.

- "Strecht [straight] up and doun, like a shit-hoose door."

- "Talking about dishes, how's your bowls" (pron. *bowels*).

- "Taste's everything, as the man said when he kissed the coo."

- "The Auld [old] Enemy": time.

- "The Big Nail": where mislaid articles of clothing are presumed to be hanging—that is, on the floor.

- "The grave's greedy": people who haven't long to live become even more parsimonious.

- "The Hen's March to the Midden": going in single file.

- "There's raisins [reasons] for everything and currants in dumplins."

- "They'd skin a louse [pron. *looss*] for the tally [tallow] o't."

- "Tinkers' tartan": the mottled appearance of the skin of your legs brought about by toasting them too often in front of the fire.

- "Tramp on a shit and it'll aye [always] get the braider [broader]": a warning against talking scandal.

- "Upside-doon-Jean-Dick!"

- "Up before your claes are on!" Said to anyone who is seen in the morning earlier than usual.

- "Ye've a tongue that would clip cloots [cut cloths]!" Said to anyone who's too talkative.

- "Yin o' thae eaten-and-spewed characters!"

- "Yince-errant [once-errand]. One undertaken for one specific purpose and no other.

- "Ye'd think they couldnie say 'shite' for a shilling!"

- "Ye'll a' agree in less room!"

- "Ye've got it in front o' ye, like the man wi' the big nose."

- "You've a face that would frichten the French"—or "stop a clock."

- "Your een's [eyes are] your merchant": *i.e.*, your judge when you buy anything.

- "Whae's [who's] 'she'?" "The cat's auntie." This is a question and answer made if someone uses the word 'she' when a proper or more respectful name is called for.

- "Where there's reek [smoke, vapour], there's heat, as the taid [toad] said when it shit on the ice."

- "Ye look like something that's fell fae [fallen from] the back o' a flittin' [removal]."

- "You'll be a man before your mother."

The word "belly" is used so much that it deserves a special section all to itself:

- "I have a sair [sore] belly."

- "Never make a god o' your belly."

- "Never make a midden [dunghill] o' your belly."

- "Your een [eyes] are bigger than your belly."

- "What's in your belly'll no be in your testament."

- "If I had a belly like yours I'd tie it to a tree and let the birds peck it."

And "durt [dirt]" is another word that merits mention:

- "I like kitchen [meat], no [not] a' that cookie-durt [sugar buns and cakes]."

In the Clerk Maxwell household the young scientist always had some "experimental philosophy" going forward. His results were known collectively as "Jamsie's durt."[1]

---

[1] In 1850, when Clerk Maxwell was a student at Peterhouse, Cambridge, his father wrote him a letter in which he enquired: "Did Prof. Thomson catch you, and view your 'dirt'; and if so, what thought he thereof?"

5

THE FASCINATION OF THE PAVEMENT

The kerbs and the flagstones, the lamp-posts, the shop-windows, all play their parts when the imagination of children is stirred, and games are invented. In the meditation where he more than remembers his childhood, Traherne declared: "The streets were mine, the people were mine, their clothes and gold and silver were mine. . . . The skies were mine and so were the sun and moon and stars and all the world was mine. . . ." As it happens, "All this is Mine" is a long-popular and very innocent game played by the extremely young as they run from one shop-window to the next, stretching out their arms at fullest length against the glass and claiming, "All this is *mine!*" But this triumphant age is over too soon.

Like Dr Johnson, the young acquire in time a complex about standing on pavement lines or cracks:

> ✧ If you stand on a line
> You'll break your spine.
>
> If you stand on a crack
> You'll break your back.
>
> If you stand on a line
> You'll break God's dishes.

✧ "We try to see how far we can go withoot standin' oan [on] a line."

Other diversions:

✧ "I go wi' milk in the mournin' [morning], and comin' hame wi' ma barrie [barrow], I try to overtake people that are walkin'. A [I] mus'nie [mustn't] run. Jist walk. Ye feel great when ye beat folk!"

❖ "I've often played at bein' blind, and feelin' if I could recognise the shopes in the passin'. I've even walked right through Leith Links wi' ma eyes shut."

❖ "See sometimes, I say to masel' [myself]: 'I'll make this sweetie in ma mooth [mouth] lest [last] for ten lamp-posts.'"

Besides serving some good purpose in dozens of games, the street lamp-post also makes the handiest "maypole swing." In "Giant Steps and Baby Steps," a player can even become a lamp-post! And there's the story:

❖ "This man he goes up to a lamp-post and nokes [knocks] at the wee door there, and naebody answers. He nokes and nokes and still naeb'dy answers, and he says to himsel', 'I ken there's someb'dy in, 'cause there's a light at the tope [top]'."

❖ "Pavement Twist": tobacco made up from cigarette-ends found in the street.

❖ "The Silver City": "That's where a' the gamblers gether [gather]."

❖ "The Golden Corner": "That's beside the pub—The Golden Gates."

❖ "Café de Rubber Bun": "That's a restaurant where the tea-breid's [-bread's] kind o' auld [old]."

A favourite prank in the street is to press your nose against the plate glass of some shop window (usually a jeweller's) and say:

❖ "If you vont to buy a votch buy a votch, but if you don't vont to buy a votch please take your dirty nose avay from my vindow."

Amongst the young, the most frequented shops are the "Chippie," the fish-and-chip restaurant, and the "Talley-Annie's," or ice-cream café. "Ika-da-Creme" is Italo-Scots for ice-cream, and many jibes and jokes are couched in that lingo:

❖ "Somebody throw a pea in a ma gramatophone and choka ma Harry Lauder."

❖ "Nobody wanta a chipapotata no more—go down cinemar-ama, spenda da money there."

"A Black Man" is an ice-cream slider in between two chocolate wafers. During the troubles in the Congo (1960) they were called "Lumumbas." In the 1920s the name was "A Double Event." "A Basher" is a snowball (confection) centrally placed in an ice-cream wafer. "A Ninety-Niner" is a chocolate-flake bar in the middle of a wafer or cone of ice-cream.

The chip-shop and the ice-cream café are the true clubs of working-class youths. They are run for the most part by amiable and long-suffering Italians who deserve Civil List pensions for their tact and patience. Throughout the year, scarcely a night in the week passes without some commotion in one of them—a "rammy," "blue murder," a "free-for-all," a "mickey boo. . . ."

Established and familiar supply stores come into many a joke:

The Three Laddies

✧ "Three laddies agreed that if ever they were co't by the polis, they would gie false names and the names would be the names o' shops. Yin o' the three was a wee wee laddie, and one day they were a' playin' fitba' in the stree' and a cop come along and nabbed them. Then he took oot his book and asked them their names. The first laddie said, 'Peter Allan [a drapery store]' and the second laddie said, 'Patrick Thomson' [another drapery store], and the wee wee laddie said, 'Edinburgh and Dumfries-shire [a dairy company]'."

Long ago funerals used to attract big gatherings of children and grown-ups. These were in the days before 1914 when hearses were drawn by magnificent black horses with nodding and tossing plumes. In the Edwardian period the infant mortality figures were shockingly high, and the living children were gruesomely fascinated by the funeral of a child. Afterwards the conversation among them ran on these lines:

✧ "Did you see it?"
"Aye—what a wee wee coffin!"

Despite the falling-off in funerals, weddings continue to draw children from near and far. Before long, the cry is raised:

❖ "Poor [pour] oot! Poor oot!"

This is a request to the groom to throw money from the taxi or car-window, and for such largesse there's an immediate scramble. If nothing looks like forthcoming the cry is promptly altered to:

"Hard up! Hard up!"

Or:

"Soor dook [sour milk]! Soor dook!"

The young bystanders also have their own words for the Wedding March:

❖ Here comes the bride
Sixty inches wide:
See how she waggles
Her big backside.

Or:

Here comes the bride
All dressed in white. . . .

❖ "At weddings in the 1890s the children when they saw anyone with a grey topper they'd shout, 'Three cheers for a white top hat!' or, 'Guid luck for a white lum hat!' "

On the eve of marriage and on their last working day, lads and lassies are often given a colourful and noisy "send-off" by their mates. The prospective brides or bridegrooms are made up and dressed up, elaborately, garishly and ridiculously, and they are frequently wheeled home in a child's go-cart or a shop barrow:

❖ "This lassie that was gaun [going] to get married she gote [got] oan [on] a bus with her pals, and they were singin' a' the auld songs, and she was dressed in a weddin' dress made o' fluffed-oot decoration paper, and she had an L-plate oan her back, and a caird at the front sayin' 'Pity poor Alec,' and she cairried [carried] a pottie [chamberpot] fu' o' confetti, wi' a couple o' wee, wee dolls stuck in the middle."

In the old days the "pattie" was filled with "saut [salt]."

✧ "A Mothers' Meeting": Any gathering in the street of women
  and girls that grows beyond a conversational number.

When a toddler perhaps stumbles over a flagstone and begins
to wail, most mothers exclaim:

✧ "Oh, look at the hole you've made in the pavement!"

And at the wonderment of this, the tears dry up.

Bright-hued "birlers [propellers on sticks]" often catch the
eye, and along the busier pavements a variety of wheeled toys
still get dragged or jerked along. But there seems to be little
scope nowadays for the older and stouter toys, and gradually
and unwillingly many have retreated to the back streets.

"Girds or girrs [hoops]" were once a prime favourite.
Rather posh wooden ones were sold in the shops. All right for
girls—but a boy much preferred a steel gird, the handiwork of
the blacksmith. This gird was guided by a steel stick which
neatly hooked on and when loose came in very handy for
rattling railings.

At one time, much to the annoyance of the passers-by, the
pavements swarmed with those low-bodied barrows called
"guiders" or "barries" or "hurlies": but modern traffic con-
ditions have drastically reduced their numbers.

"Suckers" or "sookers" are round pieces of leather with a
string or thong attached to the centre. After being moistened
or wetted, they are often used by small boys on the pavement
for raising the gas or water "tobies [caps for mains]"—with
the help of the atmosphere! Modern suckers are made of
rubber, and you can get double suckers where both sides can
be used.

"Hula Hoops," "Hi Lo," "Yo-Yo," "Pogo Sticks," "stilts,"
—each of these has had its day of fame. They fall from fashion
but none are ever entirely forgotten. Commercialism, rather
than the season, dictates their reappearances.

Except for newsvendors at their stances, and the occasional

rag-and-bone man, there are not many street-cries heard nowadays in Edinburgh. The oldest can still remember:

- "Tin Pots to Mend!"
- "Goats' Milk!"
- "Sheep's Bags, come awa'!"
- "Cauff [chaff] for Bed [bed-ticks]!"

which all belong to the 1880s; and the not-so-old may recall:

- "Finest American Apples, Threepence a Pound!"
- "Roob-le-bub [rhubarb]!"

and even:

- "Briquettes!"
- "Ca-ole!"

which belong to the 1920s, and are still sometimes heard.

Street entertainers are also a diminishing company. Such as the singers, the fiddlers and the performers on penny whistles:

- " 'Old Bob' still plays the box [accordion] in Rose Street as he has done for the past thirty years, but where's yon old violinist, with the rusty, black coat, the soft hat and the red beard? There was a legend got around that he'd come down in the world. Then there was the man with the bicycle bells and 'Spin [spoon] Willie.' The chap I mind more than anybody was a one-leggéd sailor who played the mandoline in Hanover Street."

The pipes, drums and cymbal of John Cadona's own One-Man-Band, will alas! be heard no more;[1] and another familiar figure that Time appears to have shackled is that popular escapologist—"I'm Cardinal, the Boy with the Body."

Young people who play in the street occasionally "cast oot [fall out]" among themselves and at the height of the quarrel "cry each other names" or jibe at each other with the first

---

[1] John Cadona (probably the best-known and certainly the best-beloved of Edinburgh's public personalities) died 12 Jan. 1964. But his son Tom intends to carry on with the same act.

appropriate line or rhyme that comes to mind. These jibes or retorts are occasionally directed at unusual strangers.

✧   "Balls to you, love!"

✧   "Feardie-gowk [coward], your mother wants ye!"

✧   "Ginger, you're balmy."
    "And so is your mammy!"

✧   Alice Enterkin
    Five feet four
    Has a figure
    Like a door!

✧   O Willie Nicholson,
    Ye think ye're awfie neat
    "Skinnie-ma-linkie long legs
    Umberelly feet!"

✧   "Greasy-[a]baird   [a] beard
    Penny a [b]yaird   [b] yard
    Tuppence a wee bit longer!"

✧   "Half a laddie, half a lassie,
    Half a yellie-yite [yellow-hammer]!"

✧   "Shut your legs—here's a motor comin'!"

✧   "You're only the size o' tuppence ha'penny but ye've got the cheek o' tenpence!"

Shops avoid feuds with children—especially if the shop-keepers are bulky—and possess good rhyming names:

    ✧   Mr Barr
        Your bum's all tar
        Your belly's [a]owre big   [a] over, i.e. too
        And ye'll no get far!

"How much are your ha'penny oranges?" was an old catch for annoying shopkeepers. It was also applied to "tuppeny pies" or "penny aipples" and today this trade is just as lively—only the prices have gone up.

◇ "Could I have a quarter of a pound of bumbees' waistcoats?"

◇ "Two ounces of tartan doodles."

◇ "Have ye any windie-watchers?"

◇ "I'd like a wee tail o' mermaid."

Bigger children have a habit of sending "wee boys" or "wee girls" on these ridiculous errands; and round the shop doors or through the shop windows they peer eagerly to see what happens.

◇ "When we say, 'How much are your penny ice-lollies?' the man says, 'A penny-ha'penny.'"

◇ "A hot jones, Mr Pie!"

◇ "I'm going to buy the shop! Got a ha'penny change?"

If a very young child goes a message [errand] to a grocer's shop and says, "It's on the line [chit]," the grocer likes to reply "The money's mine."

A less familiar sight in the street nowadays is the mother, pushing in a go-cart, a tremendous load of washing, to or from the "steamie [public wash-house]." The "dukie [pawnshop]" is also less patronised. Another name for it is the "magic wand [pawned]."

◇ "I used to go wi' this woman's ring every Friday, and get it oot again on the Monday."

Here are some of the street-greetings current during the 1950s and 1960s:

◇ "Away and raffle your onions!"

◇ "Shot, hen!" or "Shot, son!" or "Shot, cuss!"

◇ To either sex: "Dollish features, come here!" (or "Dollish dial . . .!")

◇ "What's cookin', Good-lookin'?"

◇ To a girl: "Hi doll!" Or, to a boy: "Hi, doll!"

◇ To a thin person: "Benny Beanpole!"

- To one with thin legs: "Sparrie [sparrow] legs!"

- To one with fat legs: "Tree trunks!"

- To one with severe style of haircut: "Aly Khan, the Hitler fan!"

- "Take a long walk off a short pier."

- "You've got a face like a double-bass!"

- "You're a doll—Oxydol!" Or ". . .—crocki-doll!"

- If a girl hears a boy behind her calling out "Hi, beautiful!" she may turn round and retort, "No you, shipwreck!"

- To a girl who is dressed ultra-modishly: "Ye're like the back o' a bus turned inside-out, white-washed, and stuffed wi' a pancake!"

- To a youth wearing trousers with no turn-ups and rather high above the ankles: "Has your cat dee'd [died]? Your troosers is at half-mast!" Any youth worth his salt will then retort: "Yes, it fell into a river, I jumped in to save it, and they shrunk!"

- "What's that ye're wearin'? A long jacket or a short overcoat?"

- To a girl wearing the black nylons so fashionable in 1961: "Dirty knees!" or "Liquorice legs!"

- "Ye've got a figure like a match-stick wi' the wood scraped off."

- To those whose clothes are too young or too posh for them: "Mutton dressed up as lamb!"

- To anyone who grabs a seat in a bus or public hall before the person who has the best claim to it: "Would you take my grave as quick?"

"They have said, and they will say, let them be saying." These are all sort of sayings which are to be heard on various occasions. On going to the pictures:

- "Ye go in wi' a cardigan, and ye come oot wi' a jumper [*i.e.* a flea]."

- "Ye're itchin' to get in, and scratchin' to get oot."

- "Ye go in wi' an overcoat, and come oot wi' a waistcoat."

In front of a shop-window (an alphabetic guessing-game):

> "I spy with my little eye
  Something beginning with *A*. . . ."

In the bus, young passengers often play a game based on association and naming things seen in the passing streetscape:

> "Lamp-posts, thank you."
  "Pillars, thank you."
  "Box, thank you."
  "Locks, thank you."
  "Doors, thank you."
  Etc., etc.

Bus-conductor to passengers:

> "All together—one at a time!"

And when the fare tendered to him is rather plentiful in coppers he says:

> "Ye've shairly been singin'."

> "Been playin' brag in your back-loaby?"

> "Were ye a' [at] a poor-oot wi' a bowler?"

Children scrambling out a bus or a room or a stairway or racing to some rendezvous:

> "Last oot's a hairy kipper!" or ". . . a hairy monkey!" or ". . . a haggis!" or ". . . a rotten egg!"

> "Last-one-there's a hairy monkey—but no the one that say'd it!"

Or anyone who stands in the light:

> "Ye'd make a better door than a windie [window]."

> "Is your faither [father] a glazier? He should put a windie in ye!"

Or anyone who's very tall:

> "Hand me down the moon, John—never mind the stars!"

> "What-like's the weather up there?"

> "Go on—ya long drink o' water!"

Or any girl who shouts, in a bantering way, across the street, "What's the time?".

✧ "Time ye had it—only I've no time to gie [give] ye it!"

Or anybody staring in the street:

✧ "What are ye lookin' at?"
"I dinnie ken [don't know] the label's fell [fallen] off!"

✧ "Are your eyes full—and your belly empty?"

✧ "Do you want a photie [photograph]? 'Cause it might last longer!"
"Aye, I'm printin' a horror comic." Or: "You remind me of a filmstar—Frankenstein!"

Or anyone who barges others in the street:

✧ "What the ᵃpush are ye shovin' at!"   ᵃ rhymes with *lush*

✧ "Don't push—just shove!"

✧ "Don't be sorry—be careful!"

✧ "Knock me doon and say I fell: pick me up and say ye found me!"

Whistling in the street is not so commonly indulged in, as once it was. Besides the whistling of contemporary tunes there used to be lots of short whistles, such as:

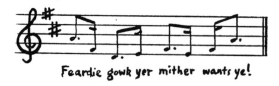

Feardie gowk yer mither wants ye!

Some of these whistles implied words that were far from proper.

Dogs nowadays have less freedom to stroll the streets, but before the age of motors, dog-owners cultivated special whistles which brought their dogs bounding back to them from far and wide. Different whistles were used for calling a brougham, a hansom, or a growler. The various trades all had their whistles too. The plasterers had one for a hod of lime ("Stookie [stucco]! Stookie! Stookie!") and the plumbers had theirs for a red-hot bolt. There was a painter's whistle which signalled the close of work: but in their shed the masons more often announced the end of their working day by hammering out this tattoo:

⌣   Stop! Stop! Stop!
      A' the masons in the shop
      Stop! Stop! Stop!

Nowadays in the street we still have the whistle for a taxi—and, of course, the "wolf whistle":

Many people talk or write about *making* children think. They have completely forgotten that thinking is a voluntary process, and that nothing comes more natural than imagination. To express this, all that a real poet requires, appears to be a blank sheet of paper, and city children, having the same, strong creative urge, can likewise work wonders with what is, after all, only the breadth of the road.

British Bulldog

⌣   Also called "Bulldozer." "Usually a boy's game, but supposing I'm the one to stand out in the middle of the road, the rest will line up on the kerb and then I'll maybe cry 'Frieda' and Frieda'll come and she'll try to charge across the road, and I'll try to stop her. I might pull her over a line or try to lift her for a count o' ten, and if I do do she's out with me, and so on, until the last person tries to charge across."

Burn the Bible

⌣   Much the same as "I'm the King o' the Castle," only the castle is a street-siver top, and as King of this grating you shout "Burn the Bible"—until you are displaced.

Butterfly Fly

✧ Also called "Fly Fly." The players line up in a row on the kerb, and their aim is to cross the street without being caught by the one that's het, who stands in front of them. The signal for running is "a word that can fly" such as "aeroplane, mavis, cricket." But if the word uttered is simply "butter" and someone has started to move, then this false starter is now het.

Catch-a-Kiss

✧ Also called "Kissiecatch," or "Kissiecatchie," or "Catchkissie" or "Catchiekissie." "Say there's a whole lot o' boys and there's the same amount o' girls, the girls have got to run away and the boys have got to catch them, and when they catch them they've got to kiss them, and after all the girls are caught and kissed, the boys run away and the girls have to catch them and kiss them."

Catch the Salmon

✧ "Two laddies take a rope and the rest o' yaes [you] run away and they try to catch ye. The last one oot's the winner. Lassies play an' a'." This is the old game of "Press-Gang."

Chicken

✧ One boy stands at a distance from other boys—with his bicycle placed cross-wise in front of him. The other boys mount their bikes and race towards the standing boy. If he moves away, he's chicken; if they brake and pull up, they're chicken.

Cigarettes

✧ "There's one person who's the Boss and maybe five others. One other person is chosen to be leader o' thae [those] five and gies [gives] himsel' and the others the names o' the different brands of cigarettes. The Boss then turns his back on the others, who line up in their places in a row, and now he cries the names o' the different cigarettes. When he comes to one o' the names picked, that person wi' the name runs up, touches his arm, and keeps on running to a wall or mark, and so does the Boss, and if the Cigarettes get to the wall or mark before him—he's oot."

Similar to "Cigarettes" are "Film-Stars," "Football Players," and "Whiskys."

Cockie Leekie[1]

❖ "There's an outer standing in the middle of the road and there's a line. The outer shouts somebody's name and this person has to run across the road without being caught. If they get across they shout 'Cockie Leekie,' which allows everybody else to run across, but if they're caught they have to help the the outer to catch the rest. Each one in turn caught by the outer gets a chance of crying the next name, and at the very end the last person has to run across the road three times without being caught. If caught he's out for the next game."

Crusts and Crumbs

❖ Played by two sides, one called "Crusts," the other "Crumbs." "There's people on one side, and people on the other side, and one that's no playin' shouts out 'Crusts!' or 'Crumbs!' Say it's 'Crusts!,' the Crusts have to run and get to their wall before the Crumbs can catch them. If any Crusts are caught by the Crumbs, they become Crumbs too, and this goes on until one side wins everybody."

Dodgie

❖ "Everybody stands round in a circle. In the centre someone stots [bounces] the ball and lets it bounce whatever way it wants and whoever's legs it goes through, then that one has to pick up the ball, first count ten and then throw the ball at somebody. If you catch it or are hit you're out the game, and the nearest to the ball picks it up and tries to knock someone else out, until, of course, only one person is left in."

Double Dodgie

❖ "Two people stand out and they have the ball (I've gien [given] ye this gemm afore) and there'll be more people standing away from them so that they won't get hit by the ball. Thae [those] two people tell what the boundaries are and if ye go beyond the boundaries ye're out the game. The two people that have the ball keep throwing it to each other and they work their way to the different boundaries, the idea of this being to get you to overstep. If ye do, ye would be just as much out as if they had hit you with the ball. Nobody else can touch the ball except these two, and the last two left are the two people in the next game."

[1] Literally, soup made from a fowl boiled with leeks.

Electric

✧ "One person is out and she can ask the rest to do anything, such as 'Climb up a lamp-post!' until she says the word 'Electric!'—but not out loud, only the shape of it, and you've all got to stop, and she picks out the best."

Fiddler's Tig

✧ "A whole crowd o' folk line up against the wa' and there's two people in the middle o' the street. One is called the Fiddler, and the other, I forget the name, you could ca' her the Number Lassie. Between them they pick a number and the Number Lassie goes owre [over] to the rest, her two hands clasped the gither [together] and held oot, as though she had the number inside. She goes fae the top o' the line to the fit [foot], seein' if they can guess it. Supposin' somebody guesses right, that person runs oot and takes the Fiddler by the hand. The Number Lassie then goes up to them and says: 'One day I went into a fiddler's shop, and I bo't a fiddle and it played like this,' and she cuts their hands apart. The two then race roond opposite lamp-posts and the first back to tig the Number Lassie is the next Fiddler. Ye cannie be the Fiddler twice runnin', so if the Fiddler wins, he gets to be the Number Lassie and the Number Lassie is the new Fiddler."

Fleur-Pat

✧ "One o' the laddies goes to the tap flett [flat] o' an entry [to a common stair], one to the second flett, one to the first flett and then on the grund flett one knocks at a door or rings a door-bell, at the same time shouting 'Fleur-pat [flower pot]!' That's the signal for the rest to start runnin' doon the stairs and to get oot that entry as soon as possible."

Fox and Chickens

✧ "Ye have as many as ye can lined along a fence or a railing, and ye need two dens, one for the Fox and one for the Witch.
There's also a Mother Chicken who stands out in the middle of the road and she shouts:

'Foxie, foxie, come home from the sea
And see what I've got for your tea.'

All the players or Chickens that are lined up take different names—Worm, Bear, Tiger, Lion. The Mother Chicken then says to the Fox, 'I've got animals for tea,' and he'll ask 'What kind?' and she'll tell him: 'Worm, Bear, Tiger, Lion.' So he'll pick one, say it was Bear, and the Bear's taken to the Fox's den.

The Mother Chicken now cries:

> 'Witchie, witchie, come home from the sea
> And see what I've got for your tea.'

The Chickens that are left have now taken the name o' flowers like 'Daffodil, Tulip, Daisy,' and the Mother Chicken'll say, 'I've got flowers for tea,' and the Witch'll ask, 'What kind?' and she'll be tellt [told] and maybe pick Tulip and the Tulip'll go to her den.

After that it could be cars was the name taken: 'I've got cars for tea.' 'What kind?' 'Ford, Vauxhall, Cadillac,' and so on, until there are nae Chickens left.''

Fruits and Vegetables

"Ye call one side of the street 'Vegetables' and the other side 'Fruits' and there's one person that stands in the middle of the road. And all the players line up say, on the Fruit side.

The one in the middle then shouts out, maybe 'Carrots!' and everyone runs to the Vegetable side. The last person over is out the game, or if the shout has been 'Oranges!' and anybody had midged [moved] they'd have been out too. The last person left in stands in the middle for the next game."

The same game is played under a dozen different titles. One is Eatables, Drinkables, and Smokables.

Giant Steps and Baby Steps

The object of this game is to cross the road from one kerb to another on the directions of the girl who's out. She stands on one kerb facing the others and she states the kind of steps and the number of steps to be taken by the players. These steps may even be directed back the way. As well as ordering various "giant steps" or "baby steps" she can also say, "Take an umbrella," in which case "you hold up your hand and twirl round." Or she may advise, "Take a minister's walk," in which case "she closes her eyes, while you go forward holding your hands like a Bible."

" 'Take a hot-water-bottle' or 'a cold-water-bottle'—that means ye either run or walk forward, while she shuts her eyes. If ye reach the kerb while her eyes are still shut, you have to turn back, so that you're often worse placed than you were before. 'A spitting kettle'—for that you spit, and where your spit lands, ye've to go there. 'A banana slide'—you slide as far as you can go. 'Scissors'—a way of crossing your legs as you hop forward."

"Take two pins" means you take two "teenie-weenie" steps, and "half a pin" is the same idea, only with one foot. "A lamp-post" means you jump while holding yourself straight and stiff, as though you were a lamp-post. For "take a bath," you lie down flat and where your head happened to touch, you move to that spot.

The player who first reaches the kerb is the winner and she stands there and dictates the steps in the next game.

"Aunties and Uncles" is similar to "Giant Steps and Baby Steps": but here you are not allowed to take a step unless you have an Auntie So-and-So, or an Uncle Somebody Else, whose names happen to be called out. If you have two of them, you can take two steps.

Gingerbread Man

◇ "Ye go along the street ringin' the entry bells and then runnin' for it."

Good Fairy and Bad Fairy

◇ "The players line up in a row while two stand out. One is the Good Fairy and the other is the Bad Fairy. The Good Fairy picks on some topic such as 'Streets' or 'Colours of Flowers.' Supposing it's 'Streets,' she tells the Bad Fairy, who now goes nearer the players and tells them it's 'Streets.' As she goes along the row each answers in turn and says, 'I want to be Lorne Street' or 'I want to be Iona Street' or 'I want to be Duke Street' and so on. And after that they call out, 'Good Fairy, Good Fairy, come across the river!' And the Good Fairy comes across. The Bad Fairy then tells her what streets have been chosen and the Good Fairy selects a street and the person who is that street has to race the Good Fairy to the other side of the road and back, and whoever wins is the Good Fairy and whoever loses is the Bad Fairy."

Hot Peas and Vinegar

◇ One lot of boys line up on the kerb. Some are named "Hot," some "Peas," and some "Vinegar." Three stairways at the opposite side of the road are also given these names. The one that's out then chooses to call "Hot!" or "Peas!" or "Vinegar!" and in every case there's a race to the respective stairs. The last in each race is out the game, and this goes on until only one is left—the winner—who stands out to direct the next game.

I Sent my Son

"Well, first of all, someone's out and she says, 'I sent my son to the butcher and the first thing he bought was something beginning with S.' Say I was thinkin' of 'sausages' I'd run to the kerb and try to catch the one that's out. If I do and she says, 'It's steak,' I have to go back again. But if I had 'a' thought o'steak and I hadnie caught her I'd go back and tell the others 'I think it's steak,' and we can a' try to catch her. Usually two are oot to cry the letters as that stops cheating and of course the son can be sent to any shop ye like to imagine."

Jacks, Queens, Kings, and Aces

A row of boys stand against a wall. The one who's out stands in the middle of the road, and the aim of the boys is to get to the other side—at the shout of "Jacks!" or "Queen's!" or "Kings!" At "Jacks!" you try to hop across, at "Queens!" you skip, at "Kings!" you run. And the one who's out, his business is to prevent you, while hopping, skipping, or running himself. If you are tigged by him, you must join him and help him to tig others. He can also cry "Aces!" (but not at the beginning) and at that cry you must "freeze [stand perfectly still]." If you move you're finished. Usually the rule is "No tigging on the pavement"—and boundaries must be stated—to prevent ridiculous running.

Jenny Come over the Water

"There's a whole lot of people against the wall. There's an outer and the outer says, 'Jenny come over the water skipping;' and the wall people, they all start to skip across the road, and she has to skip too and try to catch them. The one that's tigged or caught is the next out. Besides skipping Jenny can come over the water laughing, or crying, or praying, or crawling."

Jenny Wrenny

"There's Jenny Wrenny and a Shopkeeper and there's the rest o' the girls that are playing. They've to be things that ye sell in the shop. The shopkeeper chooses the shop it's to be, and say it's a butcher's, she gives the girls names like 'Sausages,' 'Roast Beef,' 'Chops,' or 'Kidneys.' They a' stand on one side o' the street and Jenny stands on the other. The Shopkeeper says:

> 'Jenny Wrenny come over the sea
> And see what you can buy from me!'

Jenny Wrenny then *hops* across to the shop and the Shopkeeper tells her it's a butcher's shop. Jenny Wrenny has to go up to the girl that's maybe the Sausages and guess that she is the Sausages. If she guesses right, the girl that was the Sausages is the new Jenny Wrenny and the old Jenny Wrenny becomes the new Shopkeeper. If she guesses wrong she has to go back to the other side o' the street, and the game begins all over again."

Mrs Brown went the Messages

✧ "Two or more different queues of players form up. The first queue is Mrs Brown, the second Sugar, the third Egg, the fourth Margarine, and so on. And there's an outer and the outer shouts 'Mrs Brown went for the Sugar,' and all the Sugars run across the road and back again, and the first back gets a point, and it carries on like that. The one that gets the most points is the winner. If 'Mrs Brown!' alone is called out all the Mrs Browns run and race. And when 'Mrs Brown and all her messages!' is cried, everybody runs and races."

My Daughter's Name

✧ The players sit in a row and the one that's out goes round them in a counting-out fashion, saying; "My daughter's name is black, black, black . . ." until at length she finishes off on one girl with the word "magic." This girl immediately begins to chase her across the road, and if she catches her, then this catcher is now "out."

But supposing the girl who was being chased manages to touch a railing on the other side of the road. In that event, the chasing girl now stands with her back to her in the middle of the road and she "clocks," that is, keeps moving her arms up and down—from twelve o'clock touching above her head right down to her sides (to six as it were) and back again. The girl at the railing has to pass under these moving arms without being touched. If she's touched she joins the row, if she's not, she's still out. "Magic" is the important word in this game and before announcing it, the girls often put in false words like "fish" or "cheese" or "margarine."

Odds and Evens

The one that's out decides and tells whether she'll shout odd numbers or even numbers. The players stand in a row and their aim is to reach the other side of the street. If it's odds and someone moves on the call, say, of "Four," then that person is out the game. The last player left wins.

Peep Peep

Otherwise called "Bleep Bleep," or "Pirates' Knots." "You get a scarf and you tie it to a pole or a railing, and you tie it in knots, and those that want to play stand in front of you, and they a' take the names o' flowers, and you shout out the name of a flower, say 'Rose,' and somebody that's Rose comes out and runs to where the scarf is and tries to get a' the knots out, while you run to the other side o' the road and back again, when of course ye cry 'Peep Peep!' and Rose has to leave the scarf if she hasnie [hasn't] managed to untie it. And the game begins a' owre [over] again—unless Rose had have got the scarf—then *she'd* have knotted it the next time."

Peter Pan said to Paul

One girl is out and the rest line up in front of her, each player holding out both palms. Behind the row there must be a kerb somewhere and in front of them further off, a wall. The one who's out goes along the row and back again, patting each palm in turn with either her right or left hand which she plays alternately and very quickly while chanting this rhyme:

> Peter Pan said to Paul
> "Which do you like best of all
> Kerb or hearthstone wall?"

The one the rhyme finished on, she has to make the choice. Then there's a race between the two from where they stand. If she chooses "kerb" she runs first to the kerb and back and then to the wall and back, while the other has to run to the wall and back and then to the kerb and back. If the "hearthstone wall" is chosen, the race is run the other way about. Whoever wins is out for the next game. Instead of "hearthstone wall," some players prefer "hard stone wall" or "old stone wall" or "old stony wall," and the saying of this vital "wall" can be held up by simply repeating the word in front of it:

> "Which do you like best of all
> Kerb or old stone stone stone . . .wall?"

And so keeping everybody guessing!

Rats, Robins, Ravens

❖ "Somebody stands in the middle of the road, if he shouts 'Rats!' if ye move ye're oot. 'Robins!' is hopping to the other side, the chaser in the middle must also hop. 'Ravens!' ye run across, he can run tae [too]."

Red Lights

❖ One girl stands on the kerb with her back to the others, who have gathered together on the other side of the street, and now have to try to cross over. The first girl counts up to ten, and then turns round sharply, crying out "Red Lights!" Anyone caught moving has to return to the pavement from which she started. The first who succeeds in stealing past the "Red Lights" girl and touching some previously-agreed wall or railing takes her place.

Sir Lancelot

❖ "The lassies stand in a row against the wall, while another stands out in the middle of the road and shouts, maybe, 'Sir Lancelot rides to a country beginning with G!' If someone against the wall thinks she's got the answer, she twice runs up to the far paling, and then comes back and tells the one in the middle what G is. If she's right, she gets the chance of standing out."

Thunder and Lightning

❖ "Ye bang on a door like thunder and run away like lightning."

Toot Toot

❖ Similar to "Peep Peep," only you tie a handkerchief to a lamp-post.

Toy Soldiers

❖ "Ye all stand in a ring and ye have a ball and ye start to throw or pass the ball to one another. Ye can throw it to anybody. If you let the ball drop once, you have the choice of losing an eye, an arm, or a leg. If you lose an eye, you've to shut one eye; if you lose an arm, one arm goes behind you and you must catch the ball with one hand; if you lose a leg, you've to stand only on one leg. If you lose all three, the next time you fail to catch the ball you're out. The last in wins."

Two Broken Matchsticks

Girls stand in a row, while two stand out—these are the "Broken Matchsticks." Then they recite the following dialogue:

> BROKEN MATCHSTICKS: Here come two Broken Matchsticks.
>
> OTHER GIRLS: Where from?
>
> BROKEN MATCHSTICKS: From the Land of Nowhere.
>
> OTHER GIRLS: What's your trade?
>
> BROKEN MATCHSTICKS: Lemonade.
>
> OTHER GIRLS: Start to work!

"Ye've got to do an action as if ye were working, and the other girls have to guess it. They run after ye, and they've got to catch ye before they can say what it is. If they're wrong the game goes on again. But if one o' them is right, she becomes a Broken Matchstick."

"Up and Down the Chimney-Pots" is exactly the same sort of game; and "Pale Pink Pyjamas" is similar, only it's played in teams.

Traffic Lights

"Ye've a' to stand in a circle, but one girl stands a wee bit to the side, and she calls 'Red!' and the people in the circle stand still. The last person to stand still has to sit out at the side. Then the girl calls 'Green!' and ye a' run roond and roond until she says 'Amber!' and then ye go doon on your knees. The last person to go doon sits to the side. And they keep on doing that as the girl cries oot the traffic lights until only one person is left in the circle. They've won."

Up and Down the Chimney-Pots

"Ye get them to line up against the wall, and the two people go and then select something to do and they come and one of

the people in the wall will say, 'What's your occupation?'
And we'll say 'Shy!' Then they cry 'Show me!' And you do
the action; and then if they guess right they chase you, and if
they catch you, they're out." The same sort of game as "Broken
Matchsticks."

Walk the Plank or Join the Crew

"Say there's about six people—right? Ye divide them up into
two sets o' three. Ken [know], that's the pavement there, that's
the road, and that's the other pavement. Well, they toss up,
and whae-ever loses the toss goes out on to the road, the three
o' them—they're the Crew. The other three line up on the
pavement and one o' them is asked 'Walk the plank or join
the Crew?'

To 'walk the plank' means ye've got to run across to the
other side o' the road and the Crew in the middle has to try
and catch ye and hold ye up in the air or off the ground,
anyway. And then ye're in the Crew if they dae [do] that.
If ye manage to walk the plank—that is, reach the other pavement—then the rest can run for it, too, but no before then.
Sometimes when ye're asked, ye join the Crew—if they look
a lot o' wee fellies [fellows]—ye ken, to make it evener."

What's the Time, Mr Wolf?

"One's out, and that's the Wolf; and the whole line of players
are behind him and they shout, 'What's the time, Mr Wolf?'
And if he says, 'Three o'clock,' nothing happens, but if he says
'Twelve o'clock,' well, that's his dinner-time and everybody
runs away, because if he catches one he puts him or her into
the 'dinner-pot.' Five o'clock can be the Wolf's tea-time and
nine o'clock his supper-time, if ye like."

White Horse

"The one that's het chooses something white to stand on—
white paper or white stone or white anything. He counts up
to ten and the rest keep running from one white thing to
another. One of these things is chosen as 'white horse' by the
person that's het, and when someone gets on to that, he shouts
out 'White horse!' and whoever's on it is now het."

"That's no the game we ca' 'White Horse.'"

"The 'White Horse' you're thinkin' o' is ma [my] 'Semo-
lina'."

You can't Cross the River

"One person goes into the middle o' the road and says, maybe, 'You can't cross the river unless you've got blue.' If yaiz [you] have a' got something blue on, ye can walk across, but if ye havnie [haven't], ye have to run and dodge to the other side o' the road, and if the yin in the middle tigs ye, then it's your turn o' being out and he joins the others."

6

STREET SONGS, CHANTS, AND RECITATIONS

Robert Louis Stevenson, in some telling phrases, vividly brings back what is the experience of many a student at Edinburgh University: "crowded class-rooms"; "a gaunt quadrangle"; "a bell hourly booming above the traffic of the city, to recall him from the public-house where he has been lunching, or the streets where he has been wandering fancy-free."

Within the precincts of that quadrangle, the days and the works of Aristophanes or Rabelais, may be solemnly delved into, and all this while, outside, their same, old world is even more breezily and recklessly, alive. At every corner, the wanderer glimpses still-newer views of Arthur Seat, or "The Castle of Maiden," or "Pentland's tow'ring tap." Through legend and poetry, the "nobill toun" lives right back to its beginning; as we walk under the "air-cock o' St Giles" or down "the sanctified bends o' the Bow" or along "George's Street" or the "ever-glorious Lothian Road" or "dear mysterious Leith Walk." Yet over and above history, *today*, as loudly and vigorously as ever, asserts itself. Our street songs and rhymes may be a bit of a mixture-maxture but that is only in the nature of things.

All our true poets have drawn inspiration from the living street. From them, the "Oxbridge" snobbery of many of our so-called Scots, would have come in for some bitter treatment. For the makars would have backed "The University of Rose Street," any day.

Songs

A Cannie See the Target

✦ [a]A cannie see the target
A cannie see the target
A cannie see the target—
It's [b]owre far awa'.

[a] *I can't*

[b] *over, too*

Oh bring the target nearer
Oh bring the target nearer
Oh bring the target nearer—
It's owre far awa'.

All of a Sudden

⟡ All of a sudden
A big mealie pudden
Came hurtlin' owre the hill. . . .

This is only one of a great number of verses that have been put
to the tune of Susa's March *Blaze Away*. Another begins:

Oh, what a pity
She's only one tittie
To feed the baby on . . .

Broken-Hearted we Parted

⟡ Broken-hearted we parted
At the loss of my belovéd
He was a jolly sailor
And in battle he was killed.

He had a silver sixpence
And he broke it in two
And he gave me the one half
Before he went away.

He wrote me a letter
And sealed it with his hands
And he told me not to worry
For he was coming home.

Oh were I an angel
And had I wings that I might fly
I'd go to yonder valley
Where my belovéd lies.

Caviare

⟡ *Caviare comes from the virgin sturgeon*
The virgin sturgeon's a very fine fish:
The virgin sturgeon needs no urgin'
That's why caviare is my dish.

I gave caviare to my mother
She was ill in bed with 'flu:
Now I've got a baby brother
See what caviare does to you!

I gave caviare to my sister
She was a virgin sweet and shy:
Now she stands in Piccadilly
Selling what the sailors buy!

I gave caviare to my grandma
She was nearly ninety-four:
You should hear the screams of laughter
Coming from my grandma's door!

I gave caviare to my rooster
He had close on forty wives:
Now my rooster needs no booster
See those hens run for their lives!

Students' song.

Come Tinker or Come Tailor

Come tinker or come tailor, come soldier or come sailor—
Come anyone at a' that'll take me ^afae ma   ^a *from*
    ^bfaither: ^b *father*
Come rich or come poor, come ^chairmless,   ^c *harmless*
    come witty—
Come anyone at a' that'll ^dmairry me for pity.   ^d *marry*

Singing O dear me what will I ^adae   ^a *do*
If I ^bdee an auld maid in a garret!   ^b *die*

I have a sister Kate, she is handsome and good-lookin'—
Scarcely seventeen when a laddie she was coortin':
Now she's twenty-eight wi' a son and a daughter—
And I am forty-nine, and I've never had an offer.

I can darn and I can sew, I can keep a wee
    ^ahouse tidy—   ^a pron. *hooss*
Rise early in the mornin' and get the breakfast ready:
If there's one thing in this world that would make
    me ^bawfie cheery,   ^b *awfully*
If I had an auld man to ca' me his ain dearie!

Come to the Cookhouse Door

✧ Come to the cookhouse door, boys
Come to the cookhouse door:
Fill your bellies
Fu' o' jellies—
Come to the cookhouse door!

Yon Time

✧ Do you mind *a*yon time   *a that*
When the birds shit lime
And the monkeys chewed tobackie
When the wee *b*bulldug   *b bulldog*
Wi' the leather *c*lug   *c ear*
Went owre the hills to *d*cackie?   *d void excrement*

A pail o' . . .

Tune: *The Girl I Left Behind Me*. There are other verses and
other versions, particularly one beginning: "For the captain
swore. . . ." And also the golfer's favourite:

O the dirty little pill
Went rolling down the hill,
And rolled into the bunker!
From there to the green
I took sixteen,
And then, by God, I sunk her!

Don't Go Out

✧ Don't go out with Jane any more
Don't go out with Mary:
Don't go out with girls any more—
Woops! I'm a fairy!

Tune: *Pop Goes the Weasel*.

Eight o'Clock Bells

✧ Eight o'clock bells are ringing—
Mother may I go?
My young man is waiting
For to take me out.

First he bought me apples
Then he bought me pears:
Then he gave me sixpence
To kiss me on the stairs.

I would not take his apples
I would not take his pears:
I would not take his sixpences
To kiss him on the stairs.

At last I took his apples
At last I took his pears:
At last I took his sixpences
And kissed him on the stairs.

After a spell of being almost forgotten this song is now back in favour for a clapping game.

Hang on the Bell

Hang on the bell, Nelly
Hang on the bell:
Your poor daddy's locked
In the cruel prison cell.

It's swing to the left
And swing to the right:
Tell them the curfew
Shall not ring tonight.

Ben Ghazi

Have you heard of a tale called Ben Ghazi
Where most of the fighting was done?
'Twas there that a poor British Tommy
Was shot by an old atom gun.

And laying his head on his elbow
The blood from his wound flowing red
Turning his face to his comrades
These were the last words he said:

"Oh bury me out in the Desert
Under the Libyan sun:
Please bury me out in the Desert
My duty for Scotland is done."

So we buried him out in the Desert
Under the Libyan sun:
We buried him out in the Desert
His duty for Scotland was done.

I Once Had a Boy

I once had a boy
A bonny sailor boy
A boy you could call your own:
He ran away and left me
I ᵃdinnie ken where   ᵃ *don't know*
But he left me to wander all alone.

One day as I walked
By the river side
Somebody caught my eye:
It was that boy
The bonny sailor boy
Wi' another young girl by his side.

He gave me a look
Of his bonny blue eyes
And a shake of his lily-white hand
I passed right by
And I never cast an eye
For I hate to be jilted by a boy.

Standing at the Corner

I was standing at the corner
Like a good girl should—
When along came a man
Like I knew he would.

I didn't know his name
But he smiled at me—
Now listen and I'll tell you
What he did to me.

I went home to my flat
Like a good girl should—
And the man followed me
Like I knew he would.

I went into my bedroom
And he smiled at me—
Now listen and I'll tell you
What he did to me.

I put on my nightie
Like a good girl should—
He ripped it off my back
Like I knew he would.

I got into my bed
And he smiled at me—
Now listen and I'll tell you
What he did to me.

I lay on my side
Like a good girl should—
He put me on my back
Like I knew he would.

I didn't know his name
But he smiled at me—
AND IT'S NONE OF YOUR BLOODY BUSINESS
WHAT HE DID TO ME!

Students' song. The last two lines of the last verse are shouted.

Hullo Hullo Hullo

⋄ If a man come up to you
And said "Hullo hullo hullo
You are looking very queer
Could you go a pint of beer?"—
Could I ᵃno, could I no, could I no? . . .   ᵃ *not*

The Saughton Hotel

⋄ In Embro's fair city there's flashy hotels
Wi' good board and lodgings for a' you big swells:
But the greatest of these is now in full swing—
Five beautifu' buildings controlled by the King.

There's bars on the ᵃwindies, there's bars on the   ᵃ *windows*
   doors
And great wooden benches attached to the floors:
Sure I ought to know, 'cause I've been there mysel'—
For ten years hard labour in Saughton Hotel.

I came through by train and an escort by bus
I drove through the streets with the greatest of fuss:
I drove through the streets like a Lord Mayor in state—
And never got oot till I stopped at the gate.

And at the reception they asked me my name
My age and my áddress, the reason I came:
I answered these questions, a ªscrew rang the   ªwarder
  bell
For me to bath at Saughton Hotel.

Tune: *Bonny Dundee.*

H.M. Prison, Edinburgh ("Saughton Hotel") appears to be a
highly popular subject for balladry:

⟡   One Saturday night I got in a fight
      I woke next morning with a terrible fright
      The Judge said to me "You're going for a spell
      Six months hard labour in Saughton Hotel."

      They ordered a taxi and done it in style
      They never stopped till they got to the jile
      The driver got out and rang a great bell
      And that was my welcome to Saughton Hotel.

      One Sunday morning I ordered an egg
      The jailer he thought I was pulling his leg
      He up on a table and he gave a great yell:
      "Jail birds don't lay eggs in Saughton Hotel."

      They've bars on the ªwindies and bars on the   ª *windows*
        doors
      Big, fluffy carpets on all of the floors,
      I've been to that place and I've come back to tell
      There's no place in Scotland like Saughton Hotel.

The very beautiful number-song (in Scots) printed by Chambers in his *Popular Rhymes* (1841) seems to be forgotten. Many
of these number-songs (such as "Green Grow the Rushes O")
appear to be kept alive chiefly by university students, the
version which follows being one inspired by the philosophy
of revolution.

Red Wave the Banners O!

❖ *I'll sing you one-O*
Red wave the banners O!
What is your one-O?
One is Workers' Unity and ever more shall be so!

I'll sing you two-O
Red wave the banners O!
What is your two-O?
Two, two the Workers' Hands working for a living O!
One is Workers' Unity and ever more shall be so!

Three, three the Rights of Man. . . .

Four for the Four Great Writers. . . .

Five for the Years of the Five Year Plan. . . .

Six for the Six Great Teachers. . . .

Seven for the Days of the Working Week. . . .

Eight for the Eight Red Armies. . . .

Nine for the Days of the Nine Days Strike. . . .

Ten for the Works of Lenin. . . .

I'm Gaun to the Fair

❖ I'm ᵃgaun to the Fair—   ᵃ *going*
You're no' comin' wi' me:
I'm gaun to the Fair
To dance the Hieland Laddie!

Lingle Lingle

❖ Lingle lingle lang tang
ᵃOor cat's ᵇdeid   ᵃ *our* ᵇ *dead*
What did she dee wi'?
Wi' a ᶜsair heid.   ᶜ *headache*

A' you that ᵃkent her   ᵃ *knew*
When she was alive
Come to the burial
At half-past five

A Bird's Funeral

"One day [1950], taking a short-cut by St Mary's Cathedral, I saw a number of youngsters playing on the green lawn there, very close to a wall, and as everyone looked rather sombre, I asked what was going on: Said one of them—'It's a bird's funeral'."[1]

The New Top-coat

My faither *a*bo't a new top-coat   *a bought*
A new top-coat, a new top-coat:
My faither bo't a new top-coat—
And Nellie's tore the lining.

Ha, ha, ha, ye *a*neednie rin   *a needn't run*
Ye neednie rin, ye neednie rin:
Ha, ha, ha, ye neednie rin—
Ye'll get your *b*licks *c*the morn.   *b punishment* *c tomorrow*

How the Money Rolls in!

My father makes counterfeit money
My mother makes synthetic gin
My sister sells kisses to sailors—
By God how the money rolls in!

By God, by God
By God how the money rolls in, rolls in:
By God, by God,
By God how the money rolls in!

My aunt owns a girls' seminary
Teaching young girls to begin:
She doesn't say how they will finish—
By God how the money rolls in!

My uncle's a Harley Street surgeon
With implements shining and thin:
He only knows one operation—
By God how the money rolls in!

[1] The burial of deceased budgies, extinct goldfishes, and the like, is with many children a very serious matter. Some secret corner of the back-green usually is chosen. And to make sure that the dead pet still is in its last resting-place, exhumation also is very common!

My brother's a slum missionary
Saving young virgins from sin:
He'll save you a blonde for a shilling—
By God how the money rolls in!

We've spent all our counterfeit money
We've drunk all our synthetic gin:
My sister's run off with a sailor
By God what a mess we are in!

Students' song. Tune: *My Bonny Lies over the Ocean.*

My Wee Wife

My wee wife's a bonny wee wife—
Your wee wife's a deevil:
My wee wife's a bonny wee wife—
Pop goes the weasel!

Naughty Little Walter

Naughty little Walter
Wears his wifie's clothes
Don't know what to call him
But he must be one of those.

Tune: *Mighty like a rose.*

Oh, Sir Jasper

"Oh, Sir Jasper, do not touch me!
Oh, Sir Jasper, do not touch me!
Oh, Sir Jasper, do not touch me!"
As she lay between the lily-white sheets with nothing on
at all!

"Oh, Sir Jasper do not touch!
Oh, Sir Jasper do not touch!
Oh, Sir Jasper, do not touch!"
As she lay between the lily-white sheets with nothing on
at all!

"Oh, Sir Jasper do not!
Oh, Sir Jasper do not!
Oh, Sir Jasper do not!"
As she lay between the lily-white sheets with nothing on
at all!

"Oh, Sir Jasper do!
Oh, Sir Jasper do!
Oh, Sir Jasper do!"
As she lay between the lily-white sheets with nothing on
   at all!

"Oh, Sir Jasper!
Oh, Sir Jasper!
Oh, Sir Jasper!"
As she lay between the lily-white sheets with nothing on
   at all!

'Oh, Sir!
Oh, Sir!
Oh, Sir!"
As she lay between the lily-white sheets with nothing on
   at all!

"Oh!
Oh!
Oh!"
As she lay between the lily-white sheets with nothing on
   at all!

"Immorality for ever!
Immorality for ever!
Immorality for ever!"
As she lay between the lily-white sheets with nothing on
   at all!

Students' song. Tune: *John Brown's Body*, with a variation.

Of A' the Airts

⋄ Of a' the ᵃairts the wind can blaw   *ᵃ directions*
   I dearly like the West:
   It lends the Scottish Dyes a chance
   And ᵇgies the Oils a rest.   *ᵇ gives*

A Grangemouth and Bo'ness rhyme, referring to the different
factory smells.

One Day Last Hogmanay

⋄ One day last ᵃHogmanay   *ᵃ 31 December*
   The rent-day fell on Sunday:
   And as the landlord called for it
   We slung him ᵇoot the ᶜwindie.   *ᵇ out of ᶜ window*

By nine or ten, my hairy men,
We quickly surrounded him:
And as we drew his watch and chain
We whistled "Get a hair cut!"

A burglar stole a sausage roll
The shopman saw him take it:
His fist he drew and knocked him through
The linin' o' his ᵃjaiket.   *ᵃ jacket*

Perry Como

Perry Como
Uses Omo
At rehearsal
Uses Persil
At a jazz
Uses Daz
On the pillow
Uses Brillo
At the sea-side
Uses New Tide.

Perry Como
Uses Omo
For his hair
Uses Persil
For rehearsal
Everywhere:
And his mammy
Uses Camay
And his bride
Uses Tide
And his Madam
Uses Cadum
Every day.

Sambo's Auntie

Sambo had an auntie
An auntie very poor:
One day she said to Sambo
"I'll make you scrub the floor."
Sambo did not like it
Went upstairs to bed—
Sliding down the banister
Fell and broke his leg.

O one more work for the undertaker
One more job for the tombstone-maker
In a local cemetery
On a tombstone you will see
Sambo R.I.P.

Sambo had an uncle
An uncle very rich:
One day he said to Sambo
"I'll give you two-and-six."
Sambo feeling wealthy
Went into a shop—
Ten lemonades and a bottle of beer
And off he went like pop!

Stick to Marx

✧ Stick to Marx, my hearty,
Damn the Labour Party:
Hang the rich on lamp-posts high—
But don't hang me!

End your foolish wrangles
Hear the word of Engels:
"Workers of the world unite"—
And you'll be free!

Students' song: Tune: *Keep the Home Fires Burning.*

"This rhyme I always associate with 'Bonzo's,' a restaurant of
the 1920s, that catered for students. Bonzo's was in Nicholson
Square, though it flitted afterwards to the Bridges. Plain food
was served on plain deal tables and you heard a lot of plain
speaking."

The Gundy Man

✧ Tam, Tam
The ªgundy man   ª *candy, toffee*
Washed his face
In the frying-pan:
Combed his hair
Wi' the leg o' a chair—
Tam, Tam
The gundy man.

Other versions begin "Desperate Dan, the funny wee
man. . . ." "Dan, Dan, the ice-cream man. . . ."

The Last Time I was Working

The last time I was working
I was idle all the time:
I nearly killed myself
Shifting the bricks and lime.

I walked about the job all day
Just like an anxious man:
And this is the plan that I made out
For every working man.

Lie in your bed till nine o'clock
Go to your work at ten:
Have a sleep at eleven o'clock
And another at twelve again.

Drop for dinner at one o'clock
Go up and demand your pay:
If ye get the sack, don't go back—
But have a holiday!

The Milkman's Bell

The milkman's bell goes ting-a-ling-a-ling
Ting-a-ling-a-ling, ting-a-ling-a-ling:
The milkman's bell goes ting-a-ling-a-ling—
Early in the morning.

He shouts up the stair "Are ye wanting any milk?
Are ye wanting any milk? Are ye wanting any milk?"
He shouts up the stair "Are ye wanting any milk?"
Early in the morning

They shout down the stair "No, we don't want any milk
We don't want any milk, we don't want any milk!"
They shout down the stair "No, we don't want any milk!"
Early in the morning.

The Salvation Army

The Salvation Army began to sin
So they went up to Heaven in a corn-beef tin:
The corn-beef tin began to swell
So the Salvation Army went to Hell.

The Bloomin' Sparrie

There was a bloomin' ^asparrie   *a sparrow*
Climbed up a bloomin' spout
And then the bloomin' rain came
And washed that sparrie out.

And then the bloomin' sun came out
And dried the bloomin' rain
And then the bloomin' sparrie
Went up the spout again.

Tune: *Das zerbrochene Ringlein.*

Ten in the Bed

There were ten in the bed
And the little one said:
"Roll over! Roll over!"
So they all rolled over
And one fell out.
There were nine in the bed. . . .

A number-song.

Vote, vote, vote

Vote, vote, vote for Mr Labour!
In comes Tory at the door:
Take a poker and a knife
And chase him for his life—
And we won't see Tory any more.
Shut the door!

We are the Leith Walk Boys

We are the Leith Walk boys
We can dance and we can sing
We can do the Highland fling:
We can walk along Great Junction Street
Knocking coppers off their feet—
We are the Leith Walk boys.

We Three Spivs of Trafalgar Square

We three Spivs of Trafalgar Square
Selling knickers at tuppence a pair
How fantastic, no elastic
So come and get your knickers here.

Tune: *We three Kings of the Orient are.*

When the Red Revolution Comes

❖ We'll make Winston Churchill smoke a Woodbine
     cigarette
    We'll make Winston Churchill smoke a Woodbine
     cigarette
    We'll make Winston Churchill smoke a Woodbine
     cigarette
    When the Red Revolution comes.

Free beer for all the workers
Free beer for all the workers
Free beer for all the workers
When the Red Revolution comes. . . .

Fates in store for other public figures include being made to "do
the Dance of Seven Veils," to "sweep the steps of Transport
House," to "drive an Austin motor car," and to "walk the
streets of London town."

Students' song: Tune: *John Brown's Body.*

When I was Young

❖ When I was young I had no sense
    I bought a fiddle for eighteen pence:
    The only tune that I could play
    Was *Over the Hills and Far Away.*

The rose is red, the violet's blue
Honey's sweet and so are you:
So are they that said me this—
"When we meet we'll have a kiss
And when we part we'll have another"—
That's the way to love each other.

Why was he born so beautiful

❖ Why was he born so beautiful
    Why was he born at all?
    He's no bloody use to any one
    He's no bloody use at all!

Students' song.

The Darkie Sunday School

✧ Young folks, old folks
Everybody come—
Join the Darkie Sunday School
And make yourselves at home:
Bring your sticks of chewing gum
And sit upon the floor
And we'll tell you Bible stories
That you've never heard before.

Samson was a strong man
He lived on fish and chips
He went about the Canongate
Picking up the *ª*nips: *a small whiskies*
Samson had a brother
He was strong as well
Samson went to Heaven
His brother went—as well.

Moses was the leader
Of the Israelatic flock
He went to get some water
From the bosom of the rock:
Suddenly from the multitude
There came a mighty cheer—
Instead of sparkling water
It was Tennent's lager beer!

CHANTS AND RECITATIONS

Awa' to Alloa

✧ *ª*A'll awa' to Alloa   *a I'll*
And A'll awa' the *ᵇ*noo: *b now*
A'll awa' to Alloa
To buy a *ᶜ*pund o' *ᵈ*oo.   *c pound   d wool*

A Bull biGod!

✧ As I was crossin' *ª*owre the road   *a over*
I met a *ᵇ*coo—a *ᶜ*bull biGod!   *b cow*   *c rhymes with mull*

After the word "coo," the reciter makes a sudden backward
move.

Little Dabs of Powder

> Little dabs of powder
> Little specks of paint
> Make a girl really
> What she ain't.

The Cassowary

> Once there was a cassowary
> On the plains of Timbuctoo
> Killed and ate a missionary
> Skin and bones and hymn-book too.

There She Goes

> There she goes, there she goes
> ^aPeerie heels and pointed toes: *a very small*
> Look at her feet
> She thinks she's neat—
> Black stockings and ^bmankie feet.   *b dirty?*

7

GUISING BALLADS
AND HALLOWE'EN PLOYS

In the evenings approaching the "Nicht o' Hallowe'en
[All Hallows' Even]" guisers appear on the streets of Edinburgh. The best entertainment is provided by the guisers from
the most crowded and tumbledown quarters which very often
border on the quieter, more select districts. The guisers
occasionally make door-to-door calls on their better-off and
less enthusiastic neighbours.

A blackened face and a jacket turned inside out was, at one
time, the general costume; but from the middle 1950s greater
invention has been shown, and brighter colours displayed, for
there is much more dressing-up. Among the different characters may be found ghosts, witches, beatniks, pirates, clowns,
Charlie Chaplins, cowboys, gangsters, geisha girls, and even
elephants. Masks, too, have become a greater feature, some of
them bought from the shops, but many more home-made.
Turnip lanterns are still to the fore, and fruit-bazaars in Leith
Walk and elsewhere sell them all hollowed-out and ready for
lighted candles.

- "A woman asked me what is really Hallowe'en, and A [I] said
  long ago they used to carry lanterns roond to thing'my evil
  spirits."

- "When ye sing in front o' folk, ye get a beamer [red face]."

- "If the polis [police] catches ye guisin', they send ye hame and
  take the money oaf [off] ye for the Police Fund."

- "A [I] made ma lantern look fierce, and a woman said 'Ye gave
  me a fright!' "

- "The thing A [I] like aboot guisin' is the money—and the
  laughs. Ye can hardly sing for laughin'."

- "Ye make mair [more] money in the stairs [tenements], the
  rich people are tight, and it's warmer in the houses [pron.
  hoosis] than the stree'."

❖ "I went dressed as an auld woman, and the wife that came to the door said 'We don't want any hawkers!'"

❖ "Ye get bunged oot o' pubs, but no always. A [I] went as Little Bo-peep."

❖ "A man said he would set his big dug [dog] on me. There was a huge kennel there. But actually it was a wee, wee dug, a sausage-dug [dachshund]."

❖ "We went to America House that has the big cars ootside, seven o' us, and we got tuppence between us. They had a big white hankie on the door as ye went in, and a notice, and it say'd 'Haunted Castle. Do not enter. Ghosts inside.'"

❖ "A newly-mairried couple gien [gave] us a bob each, and they tellt [told] us no to tell anybody else aboot it."

GUISING BALLADS

Blinkin' Jock

❖ Blinkin' Jock the cobbler
He had a blinkin' ᵃee,   *ᵃ eye*
He sellt his wife for a hunder pound
And that was a' his fee.

His pockets fu' o' money
His barrels fu' o' beer:
Please to help the guisers—
And we wish you a Happy New Year!

Some guisers sing of:

Blinkie Eye the coalman
He had a blinkie eye. . . .

He sells his wife for "a thousand pounds," and the second verse runs:

A pocket full o' money
A garret full o' beer:
I wish you a Merry Christmas
And a Happy New Year!

Ma Garret

✧ Come up and see ma garret
Come up and see it ᵃnoo: *ᵃ now*
Come up and see ma garret
For it's a' furnished noo.

An auld broken table
A ᵃchyre withoot a leg   *ᵃ chair*
A ᵇhumphy-backit dresser   *ᵇ hump-backed*
And a ᶜbowdy-leggéd bed!   *ᶜ bow-legged*

Other versions describe the garret as being "all furnished new"
or as possessing "stools without legs" and "chairs without
bottoms."

Good King Wenceslas

✧ Good King Wenceslas looked out
On a cabbage garden:
He bumped into a Brussels sprout
And said "I beg your pardon."

I Married me a wife

✧ I ᵃmarried me a wife, O aye, O aye   *ᵃ married*
I married me a wife, O aye, O aye:
I married me a wife
And she's the plague o' my life—
O the world must be coming to an end, O aye.

I sent her for jam
And she ᵃbro't back spam. . . .   *ᵃ brought*

I sent her for cheese
And she fell and skinnt her knees. . . .

I sent her for eggs
And she fell and broke her legs. . . .

I sent her for bread
And she fell down dead. . . .

I ᵃbo't her a coffin   *ᵃ bought*
And she fell through the bottom. . . .

I buried her in ᵃdurt   *ᵃ dirt*
And she jumped ᵇoot her ᶜshurt. . . .   *ᵇ out of ᶜ shirt*

John Brown's Cuddie

◇ John Brown's ^acuddie has a sugarallie tail   *a horse, donkey*
John Brown's cuddie has a sugarallie tail
John Brown's cuddie has a sugarallie tail
And he ^bsooks it a' day long.   *b sucks*

Tune: *Marching thro' Georgia.*

Mary Morgan

◇ Mary Morgan
Plays the organ
And her brother
Plays the drum:
And her sister's
Just a twister
And her father's
Just a bum.

Tune: *Clementine.*

Christmas is Coming

◇ Please to help the guisers
The guisers, the guisers:
Please to help the guisers—
And we'll sing ye a bonnie wee song.

Christmas is coming
The geese are getting fat:
Please put a penny
In the old man's hat.

If you haven't got a penny
A ha'penny will do:
If you haven't got a ha'p'ny—
God bless you!

Guising in Edinburgh goes on during the weeks before Christmas and right up to Hogmanay—as well as at Hallowe'en.

Rise up Auld Wife

◇ Rise up, auld wife, and shake your feathers
^aDinnie think that we are beggars: *a don't*
We're just bairns come oot to play—
Rise up and ^bgie us our ^cHogmanay!   *b give*
    c present given on Hogmanay [31 December]

Taffy

⋄ Taffy was a Welshman, Taffy was a thief
  Taffy came to oor ªhouse and stole a leg o'   ª pron. *hooss*
      beef:
  I went to Taffy's house, Taffy was in bed
  I took the leg o' beef and threw it at his head.

Hallowe'en

⋄ This is the nicht
  O' Hallowe'en
  When a' the witches
  Will be seen:
  Some o' them red
  And some o' them green
  And some o' them like
  A turkey bean!

For the witches (who worshipped Satan), Hallowe'en was one
of their most important Sabbaths.

Tramp, tramp, tramp

⋄ Tramp, tramp, tramp, the boys are marching—
  We are the guisers at the door:
  If you ªdinnie let us in   ª *don't*
  We'll bash your door in
  And ye'll never see the guisers any more!

HALLOWE'EN PLOYS

⋄ "I like Hallowe'en perties [parties]. Ye get to stey [stay] up
late and if ye make a mess o' yoursel' wi' treacle or that, ye
dinnie get a row. The champit tatties [mashed potatoes] are
great, ye get silver thruppennies and lucky charms inside them.
But the dookin' and the lassies is the best."

Here are some of the customary Hallowe'en ploys:

Dookin' [ducking] for Apples

⋄ Without using hands, each player in turn has to get one of
several apples floating in a tub of water. This may be too
frightening for small children, and there are two other versions
of the game. In the first, a chair is placed with its back against

the side of the tub. Holding a fork between the teeth, each player in turn kneels on the chair, leans over the tub, and drops the fork. The player keeps any of the apples which it spears. In the second, an apple or a scone spread with treacle or a pancake spread with marmalade is fixed to the end of a string and set swinging; and now (with hands tied behind back, and sometimes blindfolded), each in turn tries to get a bite.

Nuts in a Basin

✧ Dooked-for, like apples.

In the centuries gone by, Hallowe'en stood out as a night for the supernatural. Then and then only, by various means, it could be foretold who was to die in the coming year, or who was to marry. One act of divination is still kept alive. For this an apple is carefully and completely peeled; and then the peeling is cast over the left shoulder. When it comes to rest it should form your lover's initials. But break the peeling in the cutting, and that's the end. No wedding bells next year for you!

Hide the Apple

✧ Same as "Hide the Thimble."

Fairy up the Chimney

✧ Some willing player sits on a stool near the fireplace. He's blindfolded and told to rise and stick a poker up the "lum [chimney]" and shout "Fairy up the chimney!" He has to do this four times; and when he rises for the fourth time, the stool is swiftly pulled away and he falls back into a bucket or basin full of water.

Kipper

✧ A race between teams of wafting a paper kipper from one end of a room to the other.

Match-Box

✧ "You pass the lid of a match-box from nose to nose, and whoever lets it drop is out."

Piggie

⋄ A game, also called "Cushions," in which "ye sit on cushions round in a circle, and one girl sits in the middle, and she's blindfolded. Then one of the players in the ring imitates an animal, and the one in the middle has to find out what animal it is and who's doing it."

Step on the Bottles

"A row of bottles is placed on the floor, and someone has to step over the bottles and kiss a girl who is sitting at the other end. The person is blindfolded after he sees what he has to do, and of course sometimes ye take one or two bottles away, or put a boy at the end instead of a girl."

Hide the Thimble

⋄ Too well-known to need description but the guiding cries of "Hot!" "Warm!" "Luke-warm!" "Frozen!" and so on are in general use to help seekers to find things in everyday life.

Chinese Bowing

⋄ Everybody who doesn't know the game has to leave the room. One person is then called in and told to go on their knees and salaam as though in front of a god. At the top and foot of their salaam they have to repeat the following words: "O WAW TA NA SIAM!"

It is generally accepted that the customs of Hallowe'en are to be traced back to Druidism. The Celtic year finished on the 31st of October, it was the end of summer, and the festival of the dead. The spirits of those who had died were supposed to visit their friends, now that the winter was coming on. Their death's heads (carried as lanterns by the guisers) should therefore be welcomed with warmth and good cheer.

The civilisation we live in is, probably, the very first to believe that the dead are really dead and done for, and not having a just and satisfactory explanation concerning them, must be a great weakness at the heart of our society. The Nicht o' Hallowe'en has a natural, social importance, but besides, it must also flash a warning to our philosophers.

8

THE FOOTBALL MUSE

In a well-known anthology used in schools the most disappointing poem is certainly the one entitled "The Arsenal at Springfield."[1] When first lighted on, it raises in every young reader the highest hopes. It ought of course to be "The Arsenal at Highbury" but this must be some away game. Anyhow, the poem begins with a simple majesty:

> This is the Arsenal . . .

Then it becomes a bit strange, then rather muddled, at length completely useless from the football point of view. For it deals with a munition works, not the real Arsenal!

Although Scottish schoolboys are quite prepared to see some poetry in names like The Arsenal or Aston Villa or Tottenham Hotspur, they frankly consider their own clubs are much better named than those over the Border. And then, most of the teams that visit the capital carry such a number of extra, even more cherished by-names: Aberdeen ("The Dons," "The Granite City"); Airdrieonians ("The Waysiders," "The Diamonds"); Alloa Athletic ("The Wasps"); Arbroath ("The Red Lichties"); Ayr United ("The Honest Men"); Clyde ("The Bully Wees"); Dumbarton ("Sons of the Rock"); Dunfermline Athletic ("The Pars"); Falkirk ("The Bairns"); Motherwell ("The Steelmen"); Partick Thistle ("The Jags"); Queen of the South ("The Doonhamers"); Queen's Park ("The Spiders"); St Mirren ("The Buddies," "The Saints"); Third Lanark ("The Warriors," "The Hi Hi's"). Dunfermline's nickname evolved from "Athletic" to "Athaletic" to "Paralytic" to "Paralytics" to "Pars." "Doonhamers" comes from Queen of the South playing "doon hame [down home]"

[1] By H. W. Longfellow (1807-82).

at Dumfries; and by tradition Clyde players are generally tough and determined ("bully") though on the small side ("wee").

Of famous players' nicknames the most memorable are: "Napoleon McMenemy" (Celtic 1900s, 1910s); "Barrhead Bob" (McPhail, Rangers, 1920s, 1930s); "The Icicle" (M'Nair, Celtic, 1900s, 1910s); "The Mighty Atom" (Gallacher, Celtic, 1910s, 1920s); "The Wee Blue Devil" (Morton, Rangers, 1920s, 1930s); "Twinkle-Toes" (Napier, Celtic, 1930s). These have survived from older generations, and time will have to prove those who were in their hey-day in the 1940s and 1950s. "Tiger Shaw" (Rangers, 1940s); "Big Streamline" (Young, Rangers, 1940s, 1950s); "King Willie" (Bauld, Hearts, 1950s); "The Cat" (Younger, Hibs, 1950s); "The Gay Gordon," "The King o' the Wing" (Smith, Hibs, Hearts, Dundee, 1940s, 1950s, 1960s); "The Wee Prime Minister" (McMillan, Rangers, 1950s, 1960s).

The Heart of Midlothian ("The Maroons," "Edina's Darlings," "The Darlings of the Capital," the "Jam Tarts")[2] can always command "Hearts' Faithful," a band of supporters who will follow them through thick and thin. This happily-named football club first started playing in the Meadows in 1873. Afterwards it flitted to the "Stubble Park," a green just across the road from their present field at Tynecastle. That was in 1881. Nowadays this ground is rather awkward, both to enter and to leave, and visiting fans call it "The Hole." Heart's greatest player was Bobby Walker (1900s, 1910s). He was a brilliant dribbler, famous for his swerve.

> ✧   After the ball was centred
>   After the whistle blew,
>   Porteous got up his temper
>   And away with the ball he flew,

2 With Rangers' supporters chanting "Ran-gers! Ran-gers!" the Hearts' Faithful have discovered that the best way of countering this dissyllable is to reply "Jam Tarts! Jam Tarts!" And the Hibs, "Pen Nibs! Pen Nibs!"

> Passing it over to Walker;
> Bobby ran through them a',
> Then he diddled the goalie
> And in went the ba'!

Tune: *After the Ball was Over*

He died in the early 1930s, and what a gloomy afternoon that was, the first Saturday following his death. Outside the gates at Tynecastle, vendors, even gloomier, hawked a broadsheet elegy. Bobby Walker had already furnished his own motto, a characteristic answer he gave when some one asked him to make a little speech: "I would sooner play than speak."

In the 1920s the great hero at Tynecastle Park was centre-forward John White, and in those days a popular chant of the terracing was:

> ❖ John White, John White, John White
> Score another goal for me,
> John White, John White, John White
> I want one for my tea:
>
> I haven't seen a goal since Christmas
> And now it's half-past three,
> So John White, John White, John White
> Score another goal for me!

Tune: *Chick, chick, chick, chick, chicken*

The great rivals of the Hearts have always been the Hibernian Football Club ("Hibs," "The Hybees," "The Grass") of Easter Road. Founded in 1875, this team to begin with, drew many of their players and most of their support from the "Edinburgh Irish." The rallying-cry of Hibs is "Come away the team the colour of the grass!" and their boast, "An aulder [older] team than Celtic!" The Easter Road side certainly has a history that should inspire any football muse but the best Hibs' poem (which every supporter has off by heart) is reckoned to be "Harper, McGinnigle, Dornan, Kerr, Miller ('The Ghost'), Shaw, Ritchie, Dunn, McColl, Halligan, and Walker" (1920s). The Hibernian team also had a good run in the 1940s with the "Famous Five" (Smith, Johnstone, Reilly, Turnbull, and

Ormond), just as the Hearts shone in 1950s with the "Terrible Trio" (Conn, Bauld, and Wardhaugh). At that time, a favourite end-of-game chorus ran:

⋄ They're crowning Willie Bauld the King of Scotland
They're crowning Willie Bauld the King of Scotland
They're crowning Willie Bauld the King of Scotland
And Reilly wi' a frying pan!

Tune: *Glory, Glory, Hallelujah!*

All football followers in Edinburgh look forward to the thrilling appearances that are made by the two celebrated Glasgow clubs,[3] Rangers ("The Light Blues," the " 'Gers") and Celtic ("Celts," "The Green and White," the "Bhoys," the " 'Tic"). Just as the Edinburgh Meadows had made Hearts and Hibs, so Glasgow Green gave us both Rangers (1873) and Celtic (1887). If you can imagine ten cats playing with one mouse, then you have a picture of the merciless skill of some of the best Celtic teams. As for Rangers, they have always been so great that even "Rangers coming out" is a moment of peculiar glory. The two sides have battled together in so many historic cup finals that they're labelled "The Old Firm." Of a very famous encounter, only a single verse sings—as though it were some fragment from an old, sad, and vanished ballad:

⋄ O Charlie Shaw
He never saw
Where Alan Morton
Put the ba'!

Tune: *The Red Flag*

Celtic's Parkhead is about the only ground that can claim a picturesque name all to itself, "The Paradise." In the days before 1914, this club had a burly and wonderful centre forward called Quin (remembered in the east as "durty [dirty] Quin"). The story is told of an Englishman who found himself

3 "Celtic are identified with the Catholic interest, and Rangers with the Orange. It makes no difference that some of the greatest Celtic heroes have been Protestants. These men are accepted as honorary Catholics."—Colin Brogan, *The Glasgow Story* (1952).

in Glasgow. He thought he'd sample a football match. So he went to Parkhead and was soon greatly enjoying the game there. But hearing the name of Quin being shouted on every side, he turned to a follower standing behind him and enquired innocently: "Who is this Quin?" At once the man he spoke to became almost mad with rage: "Ye ask whae Quin is!" he spluttered out. Suddenly the Englishman found his hat being smacked down right over his eyes, along with the admonition: "Away hame and learn your history!" As an anonymous poet of the sixteenth century has commented: "Thir are the bewteis of the fute-ball."

During the last twenty years there has been a great increase in the number of songs composed and sung by the followers of football. About four hundred years ago we had the "Gude and Godlie Ballatis." These were secular songs that were altered to serve the new reformed religion. In the twentieth century this process has been reversed, and many old hymns serve the cause of football; hymns like: "There's not a friend like the lowly Jesus" or "Follow! follow! we will follow Jesus."

> ✧ There's not a team like the Glasgow Rangers
> No, not one, no, not one. . . .

> ✧ Follow! follow! we will follow Rangers
> Anywhere, everywhere we will follow on:
> Ibrox, Parkhead, Hampden or Tynecastle,
> Anywhere they lead us till the flag [or cup] is won. . . .

Today, heraldry in its old form is absolutely dead; but the clashing colours and emblems of these modern jousts and tournaments are very much alive. The cup and the flag are curiously like the Grail symbols—back again. What's more, they're understood by the majority—without having to be explained. What a subject for poetry![4]

[4] The origin of football is a matter for speculation, but it must have started from some fertility ritual. It is thought that the first ball may have been the head of a sacrificial victim, and that people believed that if they succeeded in winning it and burying it they were sure to have abundant crops. Another suggestion is that the ball was the sun, and that the goals

Meanwhile football lore continues to grow:

- ⋄ "At a big fitba' match at Tynecastle or Easter Road, say, when the crowd wave their hankies for the ambulance men to come, and then the man's taken along the touchline to the pavilion —on a stretcher, ken—well, if he's carried heid foremost he's a' right, but if he's feet foremost, he's deid [dead]!"

- ⋄ "There was this fellie [fellow] coorin' doon [huddling down] on the terracing and some'dy [somebody] said 'What are ye feared [frightened] for?' an' he said 'Thae [those] empty beer bottles fleein' [flying] aboot!' 'Away!' said the man, 'dinnie [don't] be daft, ye've nae chance o' bein' hit by a bottle. Your name has to be on it.' 'Aye, that's jist ma trouble,' said the fellie, 'ma name's M'Ewan!' "

- ⋄ "Whae [who] played for baith [both] Herts and Hibs on the same day?"
  "The band."

- ⋄ "Who was the first football fan?"
  "King Solomon. He went to see the Queen o' the South."

- ⋄ "One Saturday afternoon an American visitor stood in Princes Street for the first time, and he asked a passer-by: 'Where's this Castle of yours?' 'At your back.' 'And the Scotch Monument?' 'In front o' ye.' 'And where's "Edinburgh's Disgrace?" '[5] 'O thaim [them]! They're playin' away the day.' "

Nowadays the "Hampden Roar" has become world-wide, but the days are gone when Scotland could take on a team calling itself "The Rest of the World." Yet Easter Road or Tynecastle can still be exciting on a cup-tie day with the vendors' old cries of "Rosettes and favours of the winning

---

were the nets, eastern and western, of sunrise and sunset! At any rate, the game had, to begin with, a meaning. Like certain phases in pictorial art, sports and games could be classified as organic, geometrical, or abstract in form. Hunting and running races would fall into the organic category: but, like much modern painting, most modern games are abstract, though they often include a very necessary element of geometry. Nowadays, football is quite abstract in character.

[5] "Edinburgh's Disgrace": a monument which was never completed. In the form of a Greek temple, it stands on the Calton Hill, and was intended to commemorate the Battle of Waterloo. Also known as Edinburgh's "Pride and Poverty."

team!" or "Wear the cup-tie colours!" "Penny all the half-times!" has now changed to "All the half-times, three pence!" But that ancient proposal regarding the referee still rises up from the terracing: "Dig a hole for him!"

No popular song or rhyme about a referee has appeared so far. The best-remembered referee is Peter Craigmyle (1930s, 1940s); in his ways he was rather perjink, with his stepping this way and that way—not unlike a wagtail. He might well have inspired a flyting on the old lines:

> Craigmyle, ye peip like a mouse amongst thornes. . . .

Nicknames for "refs" are more common. A reigning referee is "Tiny" Wharton. One "whistler" of long ago had the habit apparently of awarding his free kicks, somewhat alternately, first to one side and then to the other. He got the name "One for thee and one for thou."

It is hard to believe, but, in our city, it is only within the last hundred years that football has become established in the public favour. In Edinburgh in the 1840s, "the popular game for teams was shinty, played either on the Links or Meadows or in the Queen's Park, and even sometimes on the quieter streets—without challenge or molestation."[6]

Songs and Chants of the 1950s

As I was passing Easter Road

⟡ As I was passing Easter Road
I heard a mighty roar:
I only paid a half-a-croun
To get inside the door.

Clark was in the centre
The ball was in the net,
And poor old Ronnie Simpson
Was lying in the wet.

[6] J. B. Sutherland, *Random Recollections and Impressions* (1903).

He went and tellt his grannie
She said, "It serves ye right,
For trying for to beat the boys
That play in green-and-white."

If you were passing Hampden

If you were passing Hampden
You'd hear the Hampden Roar,
When Herts were beating Celtic
Forty goals to four.

The ball was in the centre
The ball was in the net,
And poor old Frankie Haffey
Was lying in the wet.

He went and tellt his mother
She said "Ye *neednie moan   *a needn't*
Ye'll never ever beat the boys
That play in the maroon."

My Old Man's a Scaffie

My old man's a *scaffie   *a scavenger*
He wears a scaffie's hat:
He took me round the corner
To see a football match.

The ball was in the centre
Then the whistle blew
Skinny passed to Fatty
And down the wing he flew.

Fatty passed to Skinny
Skinny passed it back:
Fatty took a dirty shot
And knocked the goalie flat.

Where was the goalie
When the ball was in the net?
Hanging to the floodlights
Wi' his *breeks around his neck.   *a trousers*

There's a Team at Tynecastle

There's a team at Tynecastle
They play in maroon:
They have a wee centre
In a class o' their own.

So come all ye faithful
And listen to me:
I have a wee story,
That'll fill ye wi' glee.

The Hibs they will wither
The Rangers will die:
But up at Tynecastle
The League Flag will fly.

We'll try for the Scottish
The wee Cup and a',
Wi' Conn, Bauld, and Wardhaugh
Nae bother at a'!

Tune: *On the Top of Old Smokey.*

Sing High, Sing Low

Sing high, sing low
Wherever we go
We'll follow the Jam Tarts
Wherever they go.

We'll follow them east
And we'll follow them west
Wherever they go
They play fitba' the best.

A Team called Rangers

There is a team called Rangers
They think they are the nibs:
They sometimes beat the Celtic
But they never beat the Hibs.

They play the Hearts sometimes
And win the game with joy:
But you should see how scared they are
When they meet the Baker boy.

Hearts v. Rangers

When I was passing Hampden
I heard a mighty roar,
The Hearts were beating Rangers
Two and three and four.

Young was in the centre
The ball was in the net,
Poor old Geordie Niven
Was lying in the wet.

He went and tellt his mother
She said it served him right,
For trying for to beat the boys
Who play in candy stripe.

Hearts and Hibs

Down in the jungle
Making jam tarts:
The worst team in Scotland—
The Hearts.

Down in the jungle
Making some squibs:
The best team in Scotland—
The Hibs.

The Celts

Hail! hail! the Celts are here!
What the hell ᵃdae we care?   ᵃ *do*
What the hell dae we care?
Hail! hail! the Celts are here!

This is a change from Macpherson's *Ossian*. From the opposite
terracing it awakes the antiphon:

Hail! hail! the Pope's in jail! . . .

Willie Bauld

There's a dashing centre forward whose name is Willie
Bauld,
Whose style of play and brainwork has often been recalled:
He plays for Heart of Midlothian, the pride of all the town,
And since the day that he came there he's never let us
down.

He's the fair-haired centre forward who came from New-
craighall,
He puts the breeze up defences when he is on the ball:
You can talk about your Reillys and Paddy Buckleys too,
But our fair-haired centre forward is the better of the crew.

He switches the ball from centre to right or even left,
The forwards never slacken till the ball is in the net:
Of course you know what happens when everyone has
roared,
But the noise is mighty deafening if Willie Bauld has
scored.

He was picked for Bonnie Scotland, at Wembley was keen
to play,
And injury withdrew him, they said he'd had his day:
But he will soon be back again to show them what he
can do,
For Scotland needs a centre to really see them through.

He hasn't been playing lately, the trouble, they all say,
He cannot get his boot on because of his big *tae: *toe*
But there is one thing we are sure of, we have no fear
or dread,
He will always get his cap on that fair and clever head.

The man that replaced him, his name's on every tongue,
Was the wee blond-headed laddie, they call him Alex
Young:
The day is not far away now it's here to me it seems
When Willie Bauld and Alex Young are in the Hearts
first team.

Willie has a laddie, a bundle full of joy,
Whatever could one wish for, his first to be a boy:
Now I can tell you Hearts fans, as sure as I'm alive,
We'll have a Bauld at centre in 1975.

Tune: *The Yellow Rose of Texas.*

Hearts v. Hibs

◇   There's a team at Tynecastle,
You all know its name,
Renowned for its skill
At the old football game:

It plays in the League
And the Scottish Cup ^{*a*}tae   *^a too*
And hammers Hibernians
Every ^{*b*}Ne'er's Day.   *^b New Year's Day*

To see them score goals
It's really a treat,
They play wi' the ^{*a*}heid   *^a head*
And there's brains in their feet:
And up in attack
Whether it's hot or it's cauld
Is the pride of all Scotland—
Oor Willie Bauld.

^{*a*}Oot Gorgie they reckon   *^a out at*
That Willie's the king
And all Reilly's blethers
They don't mean a thing:
For Willie scores goals
Wi' a nod o' the heid
But Lawrie's no content
Till the goalkeeper's ^{*b*}deid. . . .   *^b dead*

When Scotland played Hungary
They played to a plan
It was thought up by Reilly
And his sister Nan:
But of that sort of plan boys
We don't want no more—
If Bauld's not at centre
The game's just a bore.

Now all you selectors
Of Scotia's team
Please take off your glasses
Of blue and of green:
The rainbow has colours
Of many a hue
But maroon is the colour
For me and for you.

Tune: *A Gordon for Me.*

After the Ball was Centred

After the ball was centred
After the whistle blew
Wee Fry got up his temper
And up the wing he flew:
He passed the ball to Baker
Who scored a lovely goal
Which found them on the winning side
With Rangers up the pole.

Tune: *After the Ball was Over*.

9

ART IN THE STREET

There are few city pavements (except the very busiest) that don't show, for nearly three seasons of the year, the signs of the peevers-artist. Whenever the crocuses start to thrust through in the parks, and the thrill of the longer light heartens everybody, the girls are down on their knees, chalking up the beds and giving each figure they make their own plain or flourishing style.

Then there are the walls! Besides the arrows of chasie and the criss-cross lines of that almost universal game of O X O, there are multitudinous other decorations. Some may have been quite recently in active service, others look long dormant. White chalk is the favourite medium for our idle (or industrious?) artists.

The shape and symbol, met with oftenest, is a heart, drawn fairly big, and containing inside it, a declaration of love, like J.S. L. M.M. This is usually followed by three kisses but the whole heart may be filled with kisses. All this is the work of the lover, J.S. Initials only are used, and then the heart is naturally and invariably pierced by an arrow—Cupid's arrow —but not in every case:

- ◇ "If ye dinnie go wi' the burd [girl] any longer, ye make a wee crack in the heart, and ye pit [put] a knife through it."
  "Aye, that's right. Usually, ye jack them in when it's gettin' near Christmas or their birthdays. Anything tae dae wi' presents."

Like the trees in the Forest of Arden, our walls are marred— and for much the same reason.

Back streets that have smooth stretches of cement or macadam are greatly appreciated by certain artists—especially children aged seven to nine who do marvellous work. Passers-by may even observe a positive rhythm of interests, the youngsters having bouts of drawing brides one week, and perhaps houses the next—provided that rain showers meanwhile have scoured the street clean. In the house-designs no two fronts are alike, some have no chimneys, some many; the same with windows: and the distribution and placing of chimneys and windows couldn't be carried out more craftily. You also get houses in hearts, and hearts in houses; as well as faces, fishes, cats, bears, trains, cars, ships, rockets. . . . One and all have the appearance of having been accomplished fairly swiftly, and very confidently. Changes made aren't covered up, the old idea and the new enhance each other, and there's no rubbing out! Many of the drawings suggest the styles of established masters from severe Holbein or exact Dürer, right on to the voluptuous sweep of Matisse, or the magic of Braque's wandering line. Paul Klee must have been greatly influenced by these street *graffiti* for you see such a lot of his candelabra trees, his types of stars, his kind of thinking:

- ⟡ "I like to draw match-stick men."

- ⟡ "A [I] dinnie chalk oan [on] ma ain stair. A chalk oan the other tenement."

- ⟡ "I draw nice women."

- ⟡ "When A lived in Spey Street A was aye chalkin' oan the wa's. We used to get kicked by the watchie [watchman]."

- ⟡ "When naebody's lookin', that's when ye start drawin' oan the wa', and when anybody comes oot the stair, either ye dae a blower [run away] or ye kid oan ye're chalkin' oan the groond [ground]."

- ⟡ "Ye sometimes draw funny faces aboot folk that have chucked ye away fae [from] their windie [window] for playin' fitba'. The crabs [crabbéd people] come oot and scrub it oaf [off]."

Nowadays you often come across notions of the space age. On a church wall, some one sketches a very big moon and opposite it, a much smaller orb which a pointing arrow makes clear is "THE EARTH." Most young people imagine that the moon is much bigger than the earth.

Nearly all the writing or printing to be seen, is taken up with the subject of love. Most statements like "JEAN L. JOHN" or "JEAN GOES WITH JOHN," are generally followed with the testimony "THIS IS TRUE" or simply, "TRUE." The passer-by may also read: "FOLLOW THIS LINE AND YOU WILL FIND OUT MY NAME." On investigation the name, more than likely, will prove to be "WILLIAMINA PIMPLE" or something like that. Some pronouncements are very downright: "I HATE SO-AND-SO" or "I LOVE ALL OF YOU." The solitary word "DEN" is one that occurs fairly frequently—if we forget "sweerie words [swear words]." In the commonest of these the letter s is very often looped the wrong way:

◇ "Ye write thae [these] words when ye're in a bad mood, nae maitter [no matter] whae ye are."

Imaginary place-names sometimes crop up, such as "STINKY CORNER" or "FUNNY AVENUE" and along with them, slogans of the day such as "NO BOMB" or "BAN THE BOMB." Names of real people or real boys and girls don't occur to any great extent. You read "I WAS HERE IN 1963" but the "I" remains unknown: similarly, you see "SET ME FREE!": but perhaps the ideal secrecy is achieved by this name and address: "MR NOBODY, NO PLACE, NO WHERE!"

◇ "Ye sometimes write something aboot your pals to make them mad but maistly ye yase [use] their initials or their nicknames."

At the Easter Road end of the town, "HIBS FOREVER! HEARTS NEVER!" is commonly seen. Nearer Tynecastle the couplet either runs the other way or it's "HEARTS EVER! HIBS NEVER!" And in the closes of the Old Town, many a scribbled rhyme greets the observant visitor:

> BEWARE OF THE GHOST
> OR YOU'LL GET ᵃLOST!   ᵃ pron. *loast*

And possibly, nearby, you'll see a skull and crossbones. Hands and skulls are normally gang signs. When chalked signs or messages are left at street corners, a circle is drawn round them to attract attention. An arrow means "Continue in that direction"; and if a number is shown with it, this indicates the paces away. A cross signifies "Don't go that way"; and a circle with a dot in the middle "Gone home."

The hieroglyphics chalked by tramps and beggars on door-ways and at street corners must be as old as Babylon. But such signs are little seen nowadays. The same can't be said of "the writing on the wall!" And no doubt when the problems of CUBA and CYPRESS have faded into oblivion, our sympathy will be sought in affairs even further afield: HANDS OFF MARS! HANDS OFF THE MOON!

INDEX OF FIRST LINES

A cannie see the target: 94.
A mole aboon your braith: 63.
A peen to see a puppy-show: 18.
A red sky at night: 62.
A red sky in the morning: 62.
After the ball was centred: 121, 132.
Alie balie alie balie bee: 54.
Alice Enterkin: 76.
A'll awa' to Alloa: 111.
All of a sudden: 95.
All over Italy: 42.
Amy Johnson flew in an airyplane: 38.
An airyplane: 24.
As I was crossin' owre the road: 111.
As I was passing Easter Road: 126.
As the day len'thens: 62.
At the Cross, at the Cross: 17, 26.
Auntie Mary: 15.
Away down East, away down West: 26.

Beware of the ghost: 135.
Blinkie Eye the coalman: 114.
Blinkin' Jock the cobbler: 54, 114.
Broken-hearted I wandered: 29.
Broken-hearted, we parted: 95.
Bronco Lane had a pain: 48.
Bluebells, dummie, dummie shells: 24.
Buffalo Bill: 16

Camarachan chew pipe-clay: 17.
Can a monkey climb a tree?: 55.
Carry a poor soldier: 15.
Caviare comes from the virgin sturgeon: 95.
Chap at the door: 56.

Chinese government: 38.
Clark Gable: 35.
Cockie Bendie's lyin' seik: 54.
Come tinker or come tailor, come soldier or come sailor: 96.
Come to the cook-house door, boys: 97.
Come up and see ma garret: 115.
Cowboy Joe: 33.
Cripple Dick upon a stick: 54.

Diddle diddle dumpling my son John: 55.
Do you mind yon time: 97.
Don't go out with Jane any more: 97.
Doun Craig's Close: 57.
Down in the jungle: 129.
Down in the valley: 31.

Eachy peachy pearly plum: 45.
Eentie teentie figgery fell: 21.
Eetle ottle black bottle: 14.
Eight o'clock bells are ringing: 97.
Ena Sharples, how about a date?: 49.
Everybody's doing it: 31.

Feardie gowk: 76, 80.
Follow! follow! we will follow Rangers: 124.
For we are the Teds o' the Kirkgate: 46.

Gantin's wantin': 63.
Ginger, you're balmy: 76.
Good King Wenceslas looked out: 115.

Greasy-baird: 76.
Green peas, mutton pies: 13.

Hail! hail! the Celts are here: 129.
Half a laddie, half a lassie: 76.
Hand me down the moon, John: 79.
Hang on the bell, Nelly: 98.
Happy is the bride that the sun shines on: 64.
Have you heard of a tale called Ben Ghazi?: 43, 98.
Hear the monkeys kickin' up a row: 25.
Here comes Mrs Macaroni: 37.
Here comes the bride: 73.
Here's tae us: 63.
Here's to you and yours: 63.
Holy Moses I am dying: 28.
House to let: 20.

I can take my tea without: 42.
I had a good job: 25.
I had a little pony: 55.
I know a Scout: 34.
I live in Chinkie China: 38.
I love a cookie: 45.
I love your hugs: 50.
I married me a wife, O aye, O aye: 44, 115.
I once had a boy: 99.
I spy: 79.
I stood outside the cemetery gate: 32.
I was standing at the corner: 47, 99.
I went to the pictures tomorrow: 32.
I widnie be a Bobby: 17.
I widnie be a German: 28.
I wish I was a Bobby: 47.
If a man come up to you: 100.
If ye dinnie go to sleep: 58.
If ye stand on a crack: 70.
If you stand on a line: 70.

If you were passing Hampden: 127.
I'll sing you one-O: 102.
I'm gaun to the Fair: 102.
I'm Shirley Temple and I've got curly hair: 46.
I'm the Monster of Loch Ness: 39.
I've got a Teddy Bear: 21.
I've got sixpence, jolly, jolly sixpence: 40.
In Embro's fair city there's flashy hotels: 100.
In Leicester Square there is a *school*: 30.
In the *dark dark* world: 51.
It's oor side yet: 16.

Jenny Wrenny come over the sea: 88.
John Brown's cuddie has a sugarallie tail: 116.
John, George, Ringo and Paul: 52.
John White, John White, John White: 122.
Join up, join up, join up Churchill's Army: 41.
Julius Caesar did a beezer: 44.

Katie Beardie had a coo: 56.
Keep hair: 59.
King Farouk, King Farouk: 43.
Kings and Queens: 27.
Knock at the door: 56.

Last night there was murder in the chip shop: 34.
Leerie, Leerie, licht the lamps: 8.
Lingle lingle lang tang: 102.
Listen to the music in the tripe shop: 34.
Little dabs of powder: 112.
Long leather laces: 19.

Lùcy Locket had a pocket: 55.

Madamemoiselle from Armenteers: 26.
Marilyn Monroe: 46.
Mary had a little lamb: 39.
Mary Kelly had a lamb: 36.
Mary Morgan: 116.
Matthew, Mark, Luke and John: 57.
Mickey the Mouse is dead: 36.
Minnie the Mouse came into the house: 36.
Monday's bairn is fair of face: 59.
Mother, mother, I am ill: 31.
Mr Barr: 76.
Mrs Brown went to town: 13.
Murder, murder, polis: 20.
My dearest darling Ducky: 50.
My faither bo't a new top-coat: 103.
My father makes counterfeit money: 103.
My love's a soldier: 15.
My man's a millionaire: 33.
My name is Sweet Jenny, my age is sixteen: 12.
My old man's a scaffie: 127.
My teacher is *balmy*: 42.
My wee wife's a bonny wee wife: 104.

Naughty little Walter: 104.
No more clay pipes: 53.
North, South: 64.

O alla tinka to do the rumba: 39.
O Charlie Shaw: 123.
O the dirty little pill: 97.
O Willie Nicholson: 76.
Of a' the airts the wind can blaw: 105.
Oh, Sir Jasper, do not touch me!: 104.

Oh, what a pity: 95.
Oh ye cannie shove your grannie off the bus: 43.
Old soldiers never die: 30.
Once there was a casowary: 112.
One day last Hogmanay: 105.
One o'clock the gun went off: 14.
One Saturday night I got in a fight: 101.
One two three four: 13.

P.K. chewing gum: 34.
Passing the sergeant: 41.
Patience is a virtue: 64.
Perry Como: 49, 106.
Peter Pan said to Paul: 89.
Please to help the guisers: 116.
Popeye the sailor man: 35.
Postie, Postie: 50.
Pussie at the fireside: 61.

Rain before seven: 62.
Rain, rain, go away: 62.
Rain, rain, go to Spain: 62.
Rainy, rainy, rattlestanes: 62.
Red and green should never be seen: 64.
Red, white and blue: 30.
Ride a cock horse: 55.
Rise up, auld wife, and shake your feathers: 116.
Rock 'n' roll is over: 46.
Roses are red: 49, 50.

Sambo had an auntie: 106.
See a peen: 64.
See a' the beists in your heid: 19.
Sing high, sing low: 128.
Something old: 64.
Stick to Marx, my hearty: 107.
Stop! Stop! Stop!: 81.

Sugarallie water: 18.
Suits the wearer: 47.

Taffy was a Welshman, Taffy was a thief: 117.
Tam, Tam: 107.
The big ship sails through the Eely-Alley-O: 27.
The big ship's name was the *Lusitania*: 27.
The Beatles are four in group: 52.
The folk in the East: 62.
The last time I was working: 108.
The Lion and the Unicorn: 61.
The milkman's bell goes ting-a-ling-a-ling: 108.
The moon shines bright on Charlie Chaplin: 23.
The night was dark, the war was over: 29.
The Salvation Army began to sin: 108.
The Twenty-fourth of May: 18.
Them that wash on Monday: 60.
There is a happy land: 42.
There is a team called Rangers: 128.
There she goes, there she goes: 112.
There was a bloomin' sparrie: 109.
There was a crookit man: 58.
There were fleas, fleas: 40.
There were ten in the bed: 109.
There's a dashing centre forward whose name is Willie Bauld: 129.
There's a new moon: 64.
There's a team at Tynecastle: 128, 130.
There's not a team like the Glasgow Rangers: 124.
They say that in the army: 40.
They're crowning Willie Bauld the King of Scotland: 123.
This is the nicht: 117.

This night when I lie down to sleep: 57.
Tramp, tramp, tramp, the boys are marching: 117.

Unless the water be boiling: 65.
Up against the wall for the London Ball: 37.
Up and down, up and down: 37.

Vote, vote, vote for Mr Labour: 109.

Watch the gab, Scab!: 47.
'Way down in Tennessee (without a shirt!): 23.
We are the Leith Walk boys: 109.
We four lads from Liverpool are: 52.
We three Spivs of Trafalgar Square: 109.
We'll make Winston Churchill smoke a Woodbine cigarette: 110.
Wha saw the Forty-Second: 14.
What Friday gets: 63.
When I was passing Hampden: 129.
When I was single I used a powder puff: 33.
When I was young I had no sense: 110.
Who stole the poultice from the bairn's scabby heid?: 25.
Why was he born so beautiful: 110.
Witchie, witchie, come home from the sea: 85.

You'll have to join, you'll have to join: 42.
Young folks, old folks: 111.